T0195813

Double Blessing

My Journey from Laos to Fishhook

Kham Kurfman and Linda Pearson

WESTBOW
PRESS®
A DIVISION OF THOMAS NELSON
& ZONDERVAN

WestBow Press books may be ordered through booksellers or by contacting:

WestBow Press
A Division of Thomas Nelson & Zondervan
1663 Liberty Drive
Bloomington, IN 47403
www.westbowpress.com
1 (866) 928-1240

ISBN: 978-1-9736-7325-5 (sc)
ISBN: 978-1-9736-7326-2 (hc)
ISBN: 978-1-9736-7324-8 (e)

Library of Congress Control Number: 2019915266

Print information available on the last page.

WestBow Press rev. date: 10/04/2019

Contents

Prologue

omething was going on. I heard people outside—lots of people. Looking out our open windows, I saw movement of unorganized and chaotic crowds. Stepping out into the street, I realized they were my classmates and their families. Sobs and cries filled the dusty streets of Khongsedone, drawing me out among them. Where were they going? We had just graduated, finishing the tenth and final grade of high school a few weeks earlier; yet, here they were, heartbroken, headed to the designated gathering point—the school.

Horrified, I watched as armed Communist soldiers herded my friends into the back of an open dump truck—no seats, no cover, loaded like cattle. Families were given no clues about their children's destination. The truck rumbled off, distraught faces looking longingly back at their loved ones. Disconsolate townspeople worked their way back to their homes, already grieving their losses.

How did I escape this? I was the only one left behind. Then it occurred to me that I was the youngest one in the class, not yet sixteen years old. That had to have been why my family was not notified to send me to the school to be hauled away.

Suddenly, nothing was the same for me. The murmurings and rumors of the past year were now a clear and actual threat. We all knew the stories, and we even witnessed one gruesome event with our own eyes: Amahit. He escaped Laos but then returned as a rebel fighter. However, the Communist soldiers caught and made an example of him. There was no trial. Communist rule assumed the accused was guilty. To make an example of him, he was first forced to dig his own grave and was then paraded through town on a wagon drawn by a water buffalo and beaten until he passed out. Speakers throughout the village blared with the announcement that this is what happened when people caused trouble for the Communist government. He was dumped unmercifully in his grave and then buried while still alive. Later, when she was in graduate class, my sister, Nang, would write a paper describing this horrific memory of Amahit.

I knew I had to get out of Laos before I turned sixteen in October. My entire family's lives depended on my getting out; I knew they would never leave me behind here in Laos if the Communists took me. It was time for a plan.

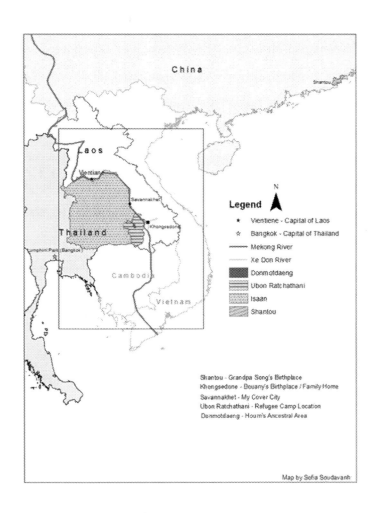

China

Shantou

Laos

Vientian

Savannakhet

Khongsedone

Thailand

Lumphini Park, Bangkok

Cambodia

Vietnam

Legend N

* Vientiene - Capital of Laos
☆ Bangkok - Capital of Thailand
—— Mekong River
······ Xe Don River
▨ Donmotdaeng
▨ Ubon Ratchathani
▨ Isaan
▨ Shantou

Shantou - Grandpa Song's Birthplace
Khongsedone - Bouany's Birthplace / Family Home
Savannakhet - My Cover City
Ubon Ratchathani - Refugee Camp Location
Donmotdaeng - Houm's Ancestral Area

Map by Sofia Soudavanh

chapter 1

Before Kham

*I*n the early 1900s, when the last king of the Laos province of Vientiane lost a war with Thailand, a large portion of Laos that lay west of the Mekong River became property of Thailand, while the area east of the Mekong remained Laos territory. The newly acquired land area in northwestern Thailand was known as Isaan. The language spoken there was also called Isaan, which was a dialect resembling Lao with a touch of Thai added. My dad's grandfather, Sone, and his wife, Thong, lived in the Don Mot Daeng District in the central part of Ubon Ratchathani, Thailand, in the Isaan region. They had supported the defeated king, so they felt targeted. Because of this, they and several other relatives emigrated to avoid the harsh treatment from the new government. All Laos citizens who stayed behind were expected to totally support the government and comply with all its laws. If anyone was caught disobeying the new government, he or she would be punished with forced labor for the rest of his or her life. This meant digging a canal in Bangkok by hand. My dad believes that some of his ancestors helped to dig the Bangkok canals.

Crossing the Mekong River to the east, they entered Laos and settled at kilometer marker 90 near Lahanam. (This was the original village named Samia, but the site is now abandoned. It's

1

now known as ລ ກ90 ("luk 90"), which means "marker 90" on Route 13.) This group settled there and remained for seven years and seven months, until a severe drought set in and they needed to move to find water. The entire family group disagreed about which direction to go, so they branched out in four different groups. One group traveled to ປາກ ຊ(Pak Suk), another headed to ເກ ງຕາວ ງ(Kengtavang), and a third went to ສະ ຫວນ (Savannakhet), which was a larger city area. Years later, one of the Savannakhet family offspring, Noutack Sithimoreda, would help my family quite significantly. My great-grandpa Sone and his immediate family decided to follow the Xe Don River to look for a place to call home. When they found a suitable location near water, they named the area ສະ ຫ(Samia), just like the marker 90 area was originally named. The town still bears the name today.

My father, Houm Sonethongkham, was born on August 14, 1934, in the village of Samia, Laos. He had two older brothers and two older sisters. His family lived off the land, farming rice for generations as well as hunting and fishing for food. Until Samia started a school, no one in the family had ever had a chance to obtain an education. Without the ability to read or write, no one could expect to have a good-paying job with the government. The military was an exception. When Laos was at war, the government drafted young adult males, even those who were illiterate, to serve their country. However, most farmers did not volunteer to enlist, opting to stay in their hometowns and continue the lives that they knew. As a young boy, my dad dreamed of being able to read, and eventually that dream came true.

In 1943, at age nine, Dad began attending a one-room school in Samia, which provided schooling only up to third grade at that time. His teacher put him in first grade and changed my dad's birthdate to 1936. This seems a little odd to us, but at the time, Laos did not have official records, and documentation could become rather random. People's birthdates were usually recorded unofficially through jotted-down notes or simply by memory of the family members. For all Dad's life, his legal birthdate remained 1936, even though he is actually two years older than this. Our younger family members could be a little more certain of their birthdates. I remember that my grandpa Song accurately recorded each child who was born in the family. He had the luxury of owning a daily calendar with one page of detail for each day. When a child was born, Grandpa Song would write down the details on that day's page and save it as a sort of birth certificate. This was as official as any certificate we could produce at that time.

My dad's brother Choung was fifteen years old when he started first grade with my dad. Imagine being nearly a fully grown man sitting side by side with six-year-old children in first grade! This shows how long it sometimes took to get any sort of opportunity for an education and how no one was turned away, no matter his or her age. After completing his third-grade education, Uncle Choung attended school in Salavan, where there were classes for first through sixth grades. He finished sixth grade and later became a policeman, eventually living in Vientiane, the capital of Laos. Uncle Choung was promoted to a high rank in the police force—high enough that ultimately the Issara Party (the new regime displacing the French-run government) felt threatened by my uncle and took him away to either retrain (brainwash) or eliminate him. When our people were taken away by Issara, there was no communication at all. Family members would not hear from their loved one for years and would assume they were dead. This was the case with my uncle. After we had been here in America for more than twenty years, my dad received word that his brother was alive and back home with his family. He had been imprisoned all that time. Just a few years after this, he died, but at least he was with his family in Vientiane for his final years. When I look back on my uncle's experience, I am thankful that my dad's situation, as awful as it became, was not as harsh as Uncle Choung's.

From 1946 to 1949, Dad followed Uncle Choung and attended school in Salavan, where he stayed in a dorm. My grandma felt more comfortable sending her twelve-year-old boy away from home with his older brother to look after him. After sixth grade, many Laotians were finished with schooling and were prepared to enter the world of work. In 1950, Dad went back home to Samia to work with his brother tapping juice from palm trees to make brown sugar to sell.

The year 1951 had a political election. My grandpa Liam's cousin, Noutack Sithimoreda, was a descendent of my great-grandpa's family who had emigrated from the Don Mot Daeng District in Thailand. Noutack's family was in the group who had settled in Savannakhet, later moving to Vientiane. Noutack Sithimoreda came to town campaigning for a political office but also to reconnect with our family. My grandpa served as his host in Samia. While catching up with each other's families, Noutack learned that my dad had a sixth-grade education, which was rare for someone in such a small community. Grandpa saw an opportunity for Dad to continue his education and asked Noutack to take my dad home with him so that he could go to the trade school there to become a teacher. Noutack agreed to take him in. The only place to get an education higher than sixth grade was in Vientiane, which is why so few people had an education beyond basic literacy. Trade schools had limited openings. All prospective students had to take an entrance exam, and the school's enrollment was limited to approximately thirty students. Only those with the highest scores were admitted. Even if a student were fortunate enough to pass the exam with the highest score, he still wasn't guaranteed an education unless he knew someone who could host him. Schools had no dorms, so a student who lived a distance away was at the mercy of a family. The host family usually paid for his uniform, supplies, and food for the year. If any medical needs arose, the host family would tend to those expenses as well.

Furthering his education was a rare opportunity indeed for my dad. My dad was always a dreamer, even at that young age, but he added work and sacrifice to the dream to make it come true. I feel that I have inherited some of Dad's willingness to try new adventures and see new sights. I cannot understand why anyone would limit him- or herself because of fear of the unknown. If a dream is worthwhile, the dreamer should be willing to step out of his or her comfort zone to accomplish it.

My dad's ambition was to return to Samia after he was educated as a teacher and principal so that he could help provide good education in that area up through sixth grade. Dad did, in fact, do exactly this.

With his better salary, my dad built a bigger house for my grandparents. This was the home that he and my mom lived in with my grandparents and two aunts and their families until after I was born. Asian tradition was that when a person became successful, that person should care for his or her family and make their lives more comfortable. Not helping one's family would have been very wrong. The community would have shamed the person for not caring for and appreciating the ones who had raised and provided for him or her in the early years. As my dad did this, he provided inspiration for other families and children to get an education and prosper as he did. In Samia, he became the role model on how to succeed in life.

Little did my dad know at the time, but his education path in a roundabout way directed him to the love of his life, my mom.

The dream of a better life was not limited to Dad's family; Mom's side of the family sacrificed and worked to improve their lives as well.

My mother's father was born in China in 1913 and came to Laos as a refugee at age twenty, escaping from the Communist rule. My grandfather Tunsong, or Grandpa Song, lived in Shantou, China, a seaport area. His older brother, Songia, had already emigrated to Khongsedone, Laos, and he sent Grandpa one hundred silver coins to pay for his travel to join him. This money was a small fortune. Grandpa Song told us in later years that during his first year in Laos, he worked hard labor and only made thirty silver coins for the entire year. His journey began on a cargo boat from Shantou to Saigon (Ho Chi Minh City) in South Vietnam. From there, he traveled by road to Phnom Penh, Cambodia, and then on Route 13 to Pakse, Laos. He most likely was relieved to be free from the oppressive Communist forces in his homeland of China, but this was not his last brush with Communism. Communism seemed to follow him around, for he eventually fled from Laos to Thailand and later to America.

When he arrived in Pakse, Grandpa Song was introduced to his uncle's widow's family. Grandpa Song's uncle had been married to a woman named Vadd (ccɔ). This uncle and Vadd had two sons named Lu (ຊ) and Lee (ບຍ), my grandpa's first cousins. Vadd (ccɔɔ) was remarried to a man named Laotiakung (ຄ ເກ ຫ ງ). They had three daughters, Houay (ບ ຢ), Lane (ລ), and Tuane (ຕ ຢ), and one son, Seuhao (ຊ ບ ວ.

Houay, my grandmother, was not the typical Chinese/Lao young lady with polite, reserved, proper manners. One reason I know this to be true is that she smoked cigarettes, which was fairly unusual for girls at that time. When I was a little girl, I once asked why she was the only grandma I knew who smoked. She described how she first began this habit. During her teenage years, Grandma's parents owned a large coffee plantation, and the coffee had to be picked by hand. They hired several workers during the harvest. Grandma's job was to track how much coffee was harvested each day. She said if no one patrolled the hired hands during the day, some of the workers would fill bags with coffee beans, dig a hole, bury the bag, and come back at night to dig it back up and sell it for their own. In order to keep them honest, Grandma would patrol the plantation on horseback. She had to wear slacks tucked inside sturdy work boots in order to keep pests such as mosquitos and land leeches off her legs. Mosquitos and giant gnats would swarm her face and neck unless she smoked. In her words, she blew that "hot air" to keep them away. Unfortunately, after the Lao Issara took over the area, her family had to give up the plantation and move back to Pakse. Grandma no longer patrolled on horseback, but she did not give up the smoking. As a result, she was hooked on smoking well into her 90s.

My mom told the story about the only time she witnessed Grandma riding a horse. A customer rode a horse from out of town and tied it to a tree in front of Grandma's store. Grandma brought water to the horse and shocked the owner by asking if it was okay for her to take a ride. To the amazement of Mom and every other villager who witnessed it, Grandma tucked up her skirt, swung up on the saddle, and took off, with everyone yelling her name as she headed down the street. Grandma Houay seemed to always be a little tougher than the average Lao lady.

I am going to speculate that the local Lao boys might have been a little bit intimidated by my hard-as-nails grandmother, but Grandpa Song did not seem bothered by her strong character. When Great-Grandma Vadd met this long-lost nephew of her first husband, she was impressed. She knew her late husband came from a good family. Grandpa Song was rugged, healthy, good-looking, charming, and, most of all, tough enough to handle a strong personality like my grandma. Vadd was so impressed that she inquired whether this fine young man might be able to marry her oldest daughter, Houay. She had been married to Grandpa Song's uncle, and this could be considered a close connection, but not actually a blood relative, just an in-law connection. Great-Grandma Vadd sought to obtain official permission for this marriage to take place. The first three elders she contacted in the community did not think this couple could get married because of their family connection. The fourth elder finally wrote down the family tree and determined there was no blood relation between Houay and Song, and they were okayed to proceed with their marriage. I am so thankful for this, because none of us would have been here if they had given up the first, second or third time they heard no for an answer; they kept going until they got a *yes*! For generations, so many members of my family persevered when many others would have quit. I feel that this persistence served us well over the years in many situations of small as well as great significance, even to the point of saving lives.

My mom, Bouany Boualavong, was born to Grandpa Song and Grandma Houay in Khongsedone on June 20, 1940. She was the eldest of eight children, four boys and four girls. In addition to these children, my grandma lost eight more children, either through miscarriage or as infants. Grandma was pregnant sixteen times, but that was common then. Medical treatments were limited and because of that, losing babies was a familiar part of life.

Like most of the population at that time, my mom did not receive extensive education. Her situation was a little different than most others. Living in the city of Khongsedone, she could have attended any of the schools there, either Laotian or Chinese, but she was needed at home to care for her younger siblings. She was raised as the daughter of merchants who knew how to buy low, sell high. My grandparents operated a small storefront in Khongsedone. A storefront means that the family ran a store from the front of their home. Their sleeping area was above the store, and the eating and living area was in the back area of the store. At that time, the only way to ensure no one would rob all your goods was to live in the same location. You could listen to know if someone was trying to come in. They sold lots of clothing, including T-shirts, buttoned shirts, and skirts. They also had dried goods and food supplies, such as rice, dried hot peppers, spices, seasonings, and so on. I remember seeing large ten-pound bags of salt, not small containers as we are used to seeing today. My grandparents would travel to neighboring towns to get items to sell, or else they might buy goods from a wholesale seller who would come through town.

As a teenager, Mom went to Pakse to stay with her grandma and her aunt in order to attend seamstress school. She learned to sew and developed seamstress skills that served her well all her life. After a couple of years, she returned to Khongsedone and began to custom design and produce clothing for people there. Grandpa had to add to his store's inventory by stocking fabric for my mom's seamstress business, so Grandpa made money selling the fabric, and Mom made an additional fee for creating the clothing for customers.

My mom could figure numbers in her head as if she had a built-in calculator. She became a very successful seamstress and trader, knowing how to make money buying and selling—a real entrepreneur who taught us all so much. Because she regretted not getting a higher education for herself, she encouraged and expected us to all succeed in the academic world. Apparently, we listened, because my seven siblings and I all attended at least four years of college, and we all showed the influence of her calculator brain, excelling in math. My siblings and I have degrees or minors in areas relying heavily on math, such as engineering, computer programming, accounting, and mathematics.

The school in Samia had been doing well for a few years, as my dad's family lived there. More grades were added so that people could obtain a sixth-grade education. Some of the best teachers were drawn to Samia to learn at this successful school. For our family, though, the school provided more than just an education; it provided the opportunity for my parents to meet. My mom's uncle Zongling had moved from China to Khongsedone, later drawing my grandpa's older brother and eventually my grandpa there too. Zongling's granddaughter, Mom's first cousin, Khamma Boualavong, and her husband, Lop Sihabouth, were teachers at the Samia school before my dad finished his schooling. When Dad finished his degree in Vientiane, he came back and took the principal position and became their boss. The couple then became matchmakers by introducing my parents, and we are so thankful to them for this.

Traditional culture should have kept my parents apart. Mom was raised in a Chinese household, according to her father's background, and Chinese usually would not consider marrying outside their own people. My grandma Houay was loyal to Chinese tradition, even though she also was influenced by Thai and Laos traditions. In a Chinese household, boys were far more likely to receive education than girls. Successful Chinese men would need to know how to use an abacus and other skills to be able to help with and eventually take over the family business. Chinese schools were almost like business schools to train the boys in the business world.

My mom only got to attend a few years of this schooling, and then Grandma needed her help at home. The main lessons girls needed to learn to perform were household duties such as cooking, cleaning, and laundry—the skills they would need in life. A girl's mother-in-law would expect her to know all the basics so that she could assist her mother-in-law and lighten the household workload. If a girl entered a marriage lacking any of these skills, this would be a reflection on her own parents, and she would not want to shame them in this way. Typically, when a girl married into a Chinese family, she broke ties with her biological family and was expected to fully engage in her husband's family. Her role was to follow her mother-in-law's training and guidance. The custom was that if a son and his wife followed the training in the business and household, they would eventually assume all the business and household possessions. Usually only one son stayed with the family business, and any other sons in the family would have to set out on their own. If the family was wealthy enough, the parents would offer financial help to get them started. Daughters usually left to join their husbands' families, requiring no more support from their parents after the wedding.

Mom's cousin Khamma, even though she was raised in a Chinese household, had broken the tradition by marrying Lop, who was an educated Laotian man. Further breaking from standard practices, Cousin Khamma also had Laotian schooling and taught home economics, which included sewing, cooking, and dancing.

Mom idolized her cousin Khamma. Every time Khamma came home to Khongsedone from Samia to pick up her salary from her boss there, she would stop in to buy supplies from my grandparents' store. Mom probably made clothing for her cousin to wear to her job. They talked and shared with one another. Khamma's married life appeared to Mom to have so much more freedom than if she had chosen to marry a Chinese man and stay in the Chinese family structure. This might have planted the beginning of a dream for Mom to also break from Chinese tradition, so later on, when Khamma and Lop brought their Lao boss to introduce to her, she was willing to consider him as a possibility.

It would not have been considered appropriate for Khamma to bring a gentleman to meet my mom, but it was completely appropriate for my dad to accompany Khamma as a customer looking to purchase supplies from my grandparents' store. After the initial introduction, Dad was on his own to pursue the relationship. He could see my mom any time he was in the area, so he would always stop in to buy supplies to take back. Tradition was that couples would not date in the sense that we would consider dating; they would not actually go anywhere together. The young man would try to find ways to show his interest, perhaps speaking to the girl at a festival or family get-together or accompanying a friend to see his sister or cousin. If the girl was receptive, and her parents approved of the young man's presence, he might continue to visit. Because my mom worked in her family's business, she often had interested young men show up at the store, but she usually left the storefront and let her parents wait on them. None of these suitors appealed to her; she must not have been looking for someone to marry before this. However, my dad apparently sparked her interest because she actually waited on him when he came to the store. My grandparents could not really control how often my dad came to see their daughter, since their store was a public business and he was a customer.

Dad probably was considered to be quite a catch with his education from Vientiane. He also dressed a little more stylishly than most of the men in the area. In fact, several Laotian ladies had pursued him, but no one seemed to attract him until he met Mom. Perhaps he wanted a little more challenge, so he pursued a relationship with a beautiful half-Chinese girl, one who came from a quite different background from him. Dad's pursuit was ultimately successful.

Mom and Dad were married on July 7, 1959, in Khongsedone. Of course, I was not a witness to this joyous event, but traditional Asian weddings are quite different from weddings in America today. During that time period, many weddings were prearranged by the families. Elders from the groom's family would approach the bride's family to suggest that their boy would be a wonderful match for the potential bride. The elders would promote their boy as a good catch for the girl, relating his best features, such as his business skills, good education, ability to provide, and good bloodline. Asians believed that a girl's mother was the indication of a good bloodline. If a girl's mother was flawed in the eyes of the groom's family, the girl would not have much of a chance of an offer of marriage to that boy.

Mom and Dad approached their relationship differently. Dad had gotten to know Mom from his visits to her parents' store, and he realized that she was probably as interested in him as he was in her, so he felt confident enough to proceed to the next step. I don't know who made the contact to inquire if Mom was interested in pursuing the relationship, but a good guess would be Khamma and Lop, or else Khamma's parents might have talked to Mom's grandma. Whomever it was, the message must have been clear that my mom was willing. Even though she was willing, her family's elders were more hesitant because Dad was not Chinese. Mom's Chinese family members would have preferred for her to marry a man who was a successful businessman with more Chinese traditions. Mom's strong will, however, had already rejected several previous inquiries, and my dad was the first one who caught her attention. Mom seemed interested in this relationship, so Dad moved on to the next step.

Dad and elders from his family went to Mom's family to

officially ask for her hand in marriage. Even though Mom's family was not in complete support of this union because of the different traditions in Dad's family, my mom was determined to make it work, and the engagement was set.

Traditionally, the groom paid a dowry for the girl's hand. Instead of considering this a simple payment to buy the girl, it was more a compliment to the quality of the girl's character. A fine girl would be worthy of a higher dowry, or as much as the groom or his family could afford. At times, the girl's family would ask a certain price for the dowry, and if the groom was well-off enough, he might even offer double the asking price. This would be one of the highest compliments he could offer his future wife and her family. If the bride's family was financially comfortable, they might return the dowry to the newly married couple as a wedding gift. If the bride's family did not have excess finances, they might use a portion of or all the dowry to pay for the wedding celebration, which lasted at least three days. The out-of-town wedding guests would arrive at the bride's family's home at least a day before the wedding, pitching in to help with food preparations and other wedding details. They would be there to celebrate the day and stay at least one more night after the wedding before heading back to their own homes. Those guests who lived close by also would show up for all the meals served. Everyone was welcome.

The day of the ceremony, the groom would get ready at his home, or if he lived in another town, he would have a host family supply a place for him. The groom would walk from wherever he got ready, joined by many people in a sort of celebratory parade, ending up at the bride's home.

At the bride's home, two beautiful centerpieces called ພາ ຂວນ (pha khuan, marigold pyramids) would be displayed there, and several traditional customs involved these pieces. The bases would be constructed the night before by a group of friends and family who were skilled in creating these centerpieces for the wedding. A single pha khuan would be created for other occasions such as a birthday, a wish to get well after a long illness or accident, a new baby, a graduation, or any good luck ceremony where a blessing would take place, sort of like a decorated cake is used in America today. The base would be put together the night before, but the beautiful fresh flowers would be added the morning of the ceremony. The centerpiece designers would go through the neighborhood, looking for pretty flowers and asking to have some to add to the creation. It was considered an honor to be asked to provide flowers for such a special occasion. Certain items were always included with the fresh or silk flowers: candles; string bracelets to tie on for blessings; long string; a basket of sticky rice; a whole cooked chicken with feet, head, and inner organs included; and eggs. Boiled eggs would always be included in the pha khuan so that a master of ceremony could break open the egg and tell the future of the couple, usually a positive prediction. After the prediction, the bride and groom would break the eggs in half and feed each other, similar to our American tradition of cutting cake and the bride and groom feeding each other. In Laos we did not have ovens to bake cakes, so this is how we celebrated. Other items could be added to the centerpiece, such as various fruits, cookies, and other tasty treats. The evening before, if girls wanted to help but did not have the artistic skills of the centerpiece designers, they would cut pieces of white string or yarn into bracelet lengths. They then would tie knots, either simple or fancy knotted designs, and attach them to a bamboo or coconut skewer in the pha khuan. These bracelets would be given to the bride and groom or anyone that you wish to bless.

A traditional Lao bride wore a bright, colorful skirt, sash, or dress rather than a white bridal gown. Her hair would be adorned with flowers or gold beads. Sometimes hair pieces were added on to provide a more dramatic look. A groom wore a colorful silk jacket. Instead of a minister to perform the ceremony as most Christian weddings use today, traditional Asian weddings were performed by a master of ceremony. The master of ceremony was usually an elder from the community who was qualified to conduct any ceremony.

Before the beginning the actual ceremony, the bride and groom would sit facing the pha khuan, each holding a long string that was attached to the pha khuan. The candles on top of the pha khuan would be lit, and all the parents, grandparents, and other family members would gather in on the floor around the couple to support them. Everyone would sit in praying position while the blessings were given. The master of ceremony chanted blessing in another language, so most of the wedding guests did not understand what was being said, but they all assumed the blessings were good. Some Laotian words were used, but for the most part, it was in a different language. If the master of ceremony was very experienced, this blessing could last for more than an hour. Laotian people were very limber and were used to sitting like this for such a long time. At one time, I could easily sit on the floor for long periods, although I have lost that skill now.

When the master of ceremony was finished with his chanted blessings, he would take two bracelets from the pha khuan and tie one on the bride and groom, saying a specific blessing or prayer for the couple. This was the indicator that the ceremony was adjourned, sort of like American culture when the minister says, "You may now kiss the bride." However, Laotian newlyweds would not show public displays of affection. Instead, at this point is when the rest of the wedding guests would grab strings from the pha khuan to place on the couple as blessings. If they wanted to give money gifts, they would attach the money to the bracelets before attaching them to the bride's and groom's arms. After the guests blessed the bride and groom, they would wander off to find the food and enjoy the celebration. The couple would have to wait patiently until every guest had a chance to tie a bracelet on and offer blessings. Tradition required the couple to keep the bracelets on their wrists for at least three days for all the blessings to be carried out. It might have been simple superstition, but who wanted to question the elders about their blessings? The bride and groom would get a chance to eat, and then the next part of the ceremony would take place.

The eldest family members and closest family friends would be called to come sit in a chair, as a couple or alone if the person had no spouse. The bride and groom would kneel at the feet of the elders and bow down to thank them for coming to the wedding and to ask forgiveness for any time they may have slighted the elders. The elders then would bless the couple and give their gift, which was usually money or gold, before leaving and allowing the next couple to come to the chair to repeat the process. The bride and groom would have a small gift like a wedding favor to give to those who give them blessings. These favors might be a candle, flower, and a little money rolled in paper or banana leaves into a funnel shape. Every family member and close friend who was older than the bride and groom would be expected to give a blessing. The guests would also bring gifts if they wanted, according to how close they were to the couple and as their finances would allow.

No one really took a honeymoon as we know it today. For three days after the wedding, the couple would reside in the house where the wedding took place. On the wedding day, a couple would be selected to perform a very honorable task: making up the newlyweds' bed for the three days. The couple would be chosen by their character, their prosperous finances, their many healthy children, and their reputation in the community. Family members would escort the couple to this freshly made bedroom to begin their new life together.

Mom and Dad's wedding celebration in Khongsedone consisted of mostly Mom's relatives. Many of Dad's family could not attend due to the distance between Samia and Khongsedone. After staying three days in my grandparents' home, they were ready to begin their married life in Samia, where Dad worked. They had another celebration there with all of Dad's family invited. This celebration provided food and a time for Dad's relatives to welcome Mom into the family.

chapter 2

Early Childhood Memories

I was born Boupharac Kham Sonethongkham on October 20, 1960, in Khongsedone. Though they were living with Dad's parents in Samia at the time, Mom traveled back to her parents' home where there was a doctor who might assist if needed during her first delivery. Asian names usually have meaning. *Rac* means love, *Boupha* means flower, and *Kham* means gold in Lao. My mom loved jewelry, especially gold jewelry. At the time, Laotians did not use a banking system; everything was cash or gold. We always lived with the fear that currency would change any time we were overthrown. We saw it happen more than once, so gold was my mom's most trusted investment. Little did we know how important it would become to our family. Gold was what kept us from starving at times and also kept us alive during some dangerous times.

I was the eldest of the eight children. Aromsack Sing was born in 1962, Kongpharack Ott in 1964, Thepharack Tay in 1966, my only sister Khantharack Nang in 1968, Seignarack Tee in 1969, Aromrac Tow in 1971, and Phomarack Noi in 1975.

These birth years are all correct. When Dad was filling out forms to come to America, he was certain of our birth years. However, he was under a little pressure to quickly complete these forms, and he was not so great at remembering our actual birth dates, especially since we did not really celebrate birthdays. He apparently picked random dates to put down for each of us. He was smart enough to write down the dates for us to memorize in case we were asked, thank goodness. We all had to state our names and birthdates when we were interviewed, so we were fortunate to know what our documents said so we could memorize the dates. My birthdate is accurate because I was with him as he filled out the forms. If Mom had gotten home a little earlier that day, perhaps more of my siblings' birthdates would have been accurate. As it was, Mom was not home before Dad had to submit the forms, and some of us have two different birthdates, the actual one and the one that Dad created under pressure.

Our first name were for school or official business. Most people would call us by our nicknames or pet names. When we came to America, we all decided to use our pet names as our middle names. Rac was my dad's idea to use in some of my brothers' names in order to have our names rhyme to some extent. When we left Southeast Asia to enter America, we ranged in age from eighteen years old down to four years old. Very few families of that size were fortunate enough to have all family members escape safely.

As children in a small village, we had a lot of freedom. When we were playing outside, we could ask any adult to go with us to the river or wherever we were heading. We never had to worry about strangers hurting us; we all watched out for each other.

Entertainment depended on our creativity. All the games we played were made-up games. We played lots of outdoor games, like skipping rocks, playing a variety of Simon Says, or jumping rope. Every day we enjoyed swimming with friends while bathing. We entertained ourselves in the shade during the hottest part of the day. At night we played hide-and-seek or set up house, playing like we had a mommy, daddy, baby, and so on. Though we were without toys or expensive items, we still had so much fun.

Mosquito nets on our beds kept the bugs off us so we could sleep. Our houses were all open without screens at the windows. At night we had to tuck the netting in tight so that the mosquitos couldn't get in. If I got close to the edge, the mosquitos could stick me through the net. Mosquito bites were more than just itchy bumps; malaria was a real childhood threat. This and other diseases took so many young lives. The best defenses were to use the mosquito netting and boil all our drinking water. Mom was diligent about keeping us safe in this way.

Even in our tiny village with no electricity, people had ways to provide lights at night using our available resources. Some of the adults would tap the resin from a tree and mix it with finely chopped dry firewood. This made a sticky consistency filler for a burning torch. They used big dried leaves to wrap around the outside of the torch until it was about the size of a small baseball bat and then secured it together with bamboo rope tied around. At night they burned the torch, placing it on a holder to keep the ashes from dropping on the floor and burning down the house. Once our evening meal was served and the house chores were done, the torch was running out and the light was out for the night. I remember waking up the next day with my nose blackened from breathing in the smoky torch fumes. If your family had a little extra money, you might have a candle or a kerosene lamp for light. Most of the city people used kerosene for light.

Thinking back to my childhood, I can remember a few different animals roaming around. I first think of the dogs we had as pets. My family always had dogs. Lots of families had chickens running free. We had ducks and ate the eggs. We had Asian pigs. They were big, but not like the pigs here on American farms. As far as cattle in Laos, we had some, but they were a different kind, not like ours here in America. There were very few dairy cows or standard beef cattle. We had water buffalo, which are bovine, not really bison. They are sort of like distant cousins to American cattle. Large and strong, water buffalo served the rice farmers as tractors, and they could be tamed to ride. People would baby them like family, leading them around to keep them tame so they could use them to plow fields. The water buffalo would graze in people's yards because there were no fences.

Another difference in our Lao animals was that we didn't have roadkill in Laos because people owned fewer cars than we see here. We did not have to worry much about vehicles running over the very few animals we owned. I had never seen deer until I came to America. In Laos, there were deer in the mountains, and some people would hunt them, but I never saw a live one. However, I did see plenty of snakes, plenty of lizards, and plenty of scorpions. Beautiful, colorful birds were also abundant. I had never seen squirrels, rabbits, or other kinds of wild animals like I see here in rural Illinois.

The yards around our homes did not have beautiful, lush, green lawns. The grass was short and seemed to be hugging the ground, never growing very tall, perhaps because of the type of grass it was but also because we worked hard to keep it short near our house. We would take a shovel out and dig to keep a walking trail clear. No one wanted to be surprised by any snakes or scorpions hiding where we walked. When we played hide-and-seek at night, we were sure to stay in the yard rather than in taller grass farther out from the house where we could possibly step on any number of poisonous creatures.

Many of the necessities Americans took for granted in the 1960s and 1970s did not exist for us. We didn't have an indoor shower, bathroom, electricity, running water, washing machine, dryer, or stove. Television was a completely alien invention to our community. Unless we had fresh batteries, we could not even listen to the radio. If we would run our batteries down, we wouldn't have any more radio until Mom went to town. However, if someone's radio was playing outside, we could enjoy the song from our house. The houses were all open. In fact, my girlfriends and I would all sit around listening to our favorite songs on the radio, and we would try to write down all the words. Sometimes one of us would take one line, the next girl the next line, and so on. When we would get the lines completed, we would check it the next time the song came on. If we had the words right, we would add it to our official songbook. Such fun! In school, we had a music class, but we were never taught to read music. As a matter of fact, I did not know there was such a thing as written music until we came to America and I tried to sing in the choir at church. I finally realized that this was how people would know how to go up or down or how long to hold each note. In music class, we listened to songs over and over and tried to mimic them. Each student had to perform an a cappella song with the words memorized. Our songbook came in handy to prepare for these performances.

Mom cooked on a small stove over an open fire. If you had a little money, you could have charcoal as a luxury. As far as groceries went, we had no refrigerator, so we bought fresh groceries and brought them home to cook. Here in America, you don't think about food; it's in the fridge and freezer, usually stocked up for several days. Over there, our food was planned one meal at a time. If a family lived in the city, the mother would rise early and head out to market to get the next meal's supplies while the children were still in bed. In a small village, the food source depended on what the father caught at that time in his fish nets or by hunting. If fishing and hunting failed, the family might have to rely on neighbors who might be willing to sell a chicken or eggs or any other supplies.

With so many children to feed, my mother always focused on the next meal and what she might need to do to get it. Mom was never able to stop this obsession; she was always thinking about fixing the next meal, even here in America where food was so plentiful and convenient. Growing up with no McDonald's or any other type of convenient food was the only way we knew. There were some restaurants, but none of us could afford them. Occasionally, some of the villagers might make extra dishes of food and walk through the neighborhood, offering to sell them to any family who might want a little extra meal or a different dish. We could never count on this on a regular basis, but we did enjoy these pre-prepared dishes now and then. Of course, it was more expensive than fixing our own meals, but we enjoyed this at times.

Rice accompanied every meal. We might have Chinese rice or Vietnamese rice. This would be rice that had been placed in water and boiled. However, Laotians usually eat sticky rice (sweet rice). To prepare this, you would soak the rice for an hour or more, drain the water, and then steam the rice for about thirty minutes. After it is cooked, the rice is stored in a rice basket rather than a pot. In a pot, it will get soggy from the steam, but a rice basket keeps it dry and helps it retain the sticky quality. I grew up eating both types of rice. My dad did not think Chinese rice was authentic rice; sticky rice was the only kind he wanted.

Our main food was fresh vegetables. We didn't have a harsh winter, so we had a longer growing season to grow quite a variety of vegetables. Mom could feed ten people two meals with one chicken. She would put lots of salt on it to preserve it. I don't think I had ever eaten a whole drumstick before coming to America. Instead, our dishes consisted of lots of vegetables with small pieces of chicken or a soup made from boiling the chicken.

Various celebrations with enjoyable activities provided so many happy memories for me. Our family celebrated Lao New Year (Boun Pi Mai) in April. In the celebration, water symbolized a cleansing for the new year, and people would pour holy water on their homes, on large or small Buddha images, on the monks, and then on everyone else. We would wish each other good health and prosperity for the new year to come. I remember canoe races, live music, and food vendors. It was such a fun time to get to see people you did not usually see.

Because of my Chinese heritage through my grandfather, we also celebrated Chinese New Year, a three-day celebration that usually fell in February. We would get three new outfits, one for each day. Shopping as Americans shop was completely unknown to us. Without a shopping mall or any clothing stores, my mom or my aunt, both accomplished seamstresses, would make clothing for us. Khongsedone was not big enough to host a New Year's parade, but Pakse had a great parade that we got to see some years. Red decorations appeared everywhere during Chinese New Year. Red represented a state of no evil—a state of happiness and prosperity. We children especially looked forward to the tradition of the elders in the family giving money in a red envelope to the kids. Superstitions guided much of the celebration. For example, we would not clean or sweep the house during the three days for fear of sweeping away our fortune.

Chinese tradition was to sacrifice food to their ancestors. I remember my grandparents would begin preparing months in advance by purchasing live chickens, ducks, hogs, or any other animals to butcher and cook for the event. Here in America, we have the shop-until-you-drop system of purchasing gifts at Christmastime, and I suppose this could be considered the same system my family adopted to prepare for these food sacrifices. We would put our hearts and souls into preparing food to sacrifice to the ancestors. The food would be placed under a sort of shrine to the ancestors, and family members would burn incense and pray to the ancestors to provide the family's needs of protection, healing, and prosperity for the year to come. If a family lost a loved one, they would dig a little bit of dirt from the cemetery to add to the vase in the shrine, and sticks of incense were stuck into the dirt in this vase. After this ritual, we could eat and then share the food with anyone who had blessed us in any way. No businesses were open, and people were eating, playing cards, visiting with one another, and generally having a great time. I really looked forward to this holiday because these three new outfits were the only new clothes I would receive for the year, and we had such fun with friends and family during these days. Even today my grandparents' family sacrifices food to their ancestors each Chinese New Year.

My family and I grew up with Buddhism, so many of our celebrations were based on the customs of that faith. At that time, I really didn't understand the significance of each *boun* (festival), but I certainly had a great time celebrating. Different festivities took place in different villages, so we got to enjoy other communities because we could walk there.

I remember celebrating Boun Pha Vet, which was a temple-centered festival that provided a popular time for new monks to be ordained. We also celebrated Boun Khoun Khao, a harvest festival similar to America's Thanksgiving, a time to be thankful for our bountiful harvest.

Boun Bang Fai, or the Rocket Festival, resembled our American Fourth of July fireworks display. Rockets were fired into the clouds to ask for rain. This was one of the rowdiest, happiest, most enthusiastic celebrations. I remember getting to stay up nearly all night, everyone partying around a stage in the temple courtyard, enjoying an especially fun event. Several community ladies of various ages would dress up in their finest and gather on the stage. Any man who was willing to donate money toward the temple upkeep would pay to request his favorite song from the band and name the lady he would wish to dance with. The music would begin, and the spotlight couple would start the dance, with everyone else eventually joining in. I remember my dad would donate for a couple of songs and ask my mom to be his honored partner, bringing smiles to us all. Since respectable young people did not really go out on dates, this was also an appropriate chance for young girls to be on display and possibly be seen by out-of-town young men, who were more than willing to donate to the temple fund in exchange for an opportunity to meet and talk with a girl who caught their eye.

Boun Haw Khao Salak (Full Moon) was when people prayed and gave offerings to the dead at the temple. Boun Ok Phansa was a festival held at the end of the monks' three-month fast and retreat during the rainy season. The monks had to stay inside during the rainy season, and this festival marked the time when the monks could get out and travel. At dawn on the first day, people made donations and offerings at the temple. In the evening, we enjoyed Loi Krathong. During the evening parades around the temple courtyard, glowing lanterns were released into the air, creating a spectacular scene. Community members built beautiful floats (*krathongs*) decorated with flowers, incense, and candles, to place in the water to pay respect to the river spirit. Boat racing also took place during this festival.

Boun Kathin was a celebration that involved people giving goods and donations for the monks at the temple. Once again, we also had wonderful feasts and a time to enjoy friends.

The That Luang Festival was a huge celebration in the capital of Laos, Vientiane. A *that* is a monument or tombstone. The That Luang is the national symbol of Laos and considered the most important religious monument. Hundreds of monks would gather to receive contributions from the people, and an international trade fair highlighted tourism in Laos.

Though I did not get to attend the That Luang Festival as a young girl because it was so far from my home, I did attend another monument festival, Wat Phou Festival, in Champasak, located in the southern part of Laos, near my home. Champasak is the site of many temple ruins with sacred inscriptions and carvings remaining. *Wat* (temple) *Phou* (mount) *Temple* literally means "Temple on the Mount," and this was the particular temple celebrated with this festival. Dance, music, and food were always part of the fun, and this festival also included buffalo fighting and elephant racing along with the traditional activities. When I attended with my parents, I was close enough to touch an elephant and even ride one.

When I was young, we didn't celebrate birthdays. So many people did not know what day they were born, but maybe they knew the year. Most of the time the mother didn't even remember the exact day a child was born. We did not have a party or gifts. Most of us had no money or gifts to give. I see today on social media that this culture in Laos has been changing, and often birthdays are recognized and celebrated with food, cake, and parties just like we do here.

Americans today may consider my life growing up in Laos as a life of deprivation compared to life in the Western world, but I never felt that way. When a person is not aware of what he does not have, he will not miss it. We were safe and always had enough to eat. With a loving family and fun friends, I always had plenty of things to do to occupy my time. Even when threats and danger entered our lives along the way, as long as we were together, we had joy in our lives. Material possessions paled in comparison with the security and safety of our loved ones gathered around us.

chapter 3

Lao Schooling

*I*n Laos, school was a privilege. No officials would penalize anyone for not attending school. Sometimes kids would go to school just long enough to read and write, and then they would drop out to stay home and work. Sometimes it was just too hard to get to school because of the distance.

Our family would not lose out on the opportunity to learn. My dad made schooling a priority. Dad always said, "If you don't do well in school, you are not doing your job." We believed him and seriously applied ourselves in school, earnestly trying our best to do our job.

School in Laos during my childhood was like school here in many ways but different in others. We followed the French schooling system because France controlled our country. In France, children aged three to five could attend L'école Maternelle, which was a type of preschool. My village was too small to offer this.

I remember looking longingly at the schoolyard, watching the kids playing at recess and wanting to attend school before I was old enough to go. Even though I was too young to enroll, my parents got me the white-and-blue uniform so that I could walk into the school and stay at least for a little while each day. Usually I would attend for just a few hours—until recess time.

Then I was done for the day. Because we lived right by the school, my mom or one of the students would walk me home after the recess. I suppose this was a perk for being one of the boss's kids. Eventually I was old enough to attend school as a legitimate, enrolled student where I was taught most of the usual subjects found in schools anywhere.

The next level of schooling in France was L'école Primaire, which started with first grade at about six years old and continued through sixth grade (like primary school in America). All Laotians were offered this level of schooling. The majority of the population considered this a completed education. After completing sixth grade, a student could read, write, and do basic math calculations, so he or she could function adequately for the most part in Laos. At the end of the sixth-grade school year, all students had to pass a test to obtain their diplomas and to be considered graduates. When my dad was this age, someone with a sixth-grade education could become a teacher. By the time my generation finished sixth grade, more schooling was required to become a teacher, nurse, doctor, banker, engineer, or other professional. Several other types of careers, such as farming, merchant, military, and so on, were possibilities, even without extra education. The military would draft young adult men to serve their country, even though they might be illiterate. However, higher education offered a better chance to move into higher ranks and most likely earn a higher salary.

As a student, you selected your preferred field of study, perhaps teaching, nursing, or regular high school with general education classes, and you were required to travel to the test site location for that school. Each school would only take a certain number of students, and only the highest scores were accepted to fill those open spots. Each test was offered only once a year; if you did not achieve a high enough score, you would need to retake some classes, find a private tutor, or do whatever you could to prepare for the test next year. This sometimes resulted in high school classes composed of students of varying ages, due to a few who had to study for a year or two to gain admission.

If you intended to seek further education, you would be required to take entrance tests for le collège (French middle school), as well as to be placed in specific career training such as teaching, nursing, or the police force. Le collège consisted of four years of higher education to prepare students for even higher-level careers with the government. These students would be destined to become leaders in their professions. This is the path I was choosing to go in preparation to enter a program to become a doctor one day. The classes were challenging with advanced math, science, geography, and such. Even though this program was offered there in Khongsedone, and my brother Sing was attending there, my mom really wanted me to move to Kengkok to go to le collège. In addition to taking classes to further my education, I would also learn how to buy and sell from the best, my uncle Mong and his wife, Boualasy, who had a store at their home and a stand at the market. I learned a lot in the academic world from two years of classes at the le collège, but I also learned so much in the real world from my aunt and uncle. I came out of my shell and gained confidence as I was trained in how to treat customers and how to buy and sell for a profit. This knowledge was crucial later when Dad's income was cut off, and Mom had to become the main breadwinner. I could step in as her right-hand assistant and help keep the family clothed and fed.

The only picture of me at this age (actually, the only picture I have from my childhood) was randomly given years later to my mom at a temple festival in Minnesota when Mom was visiting my sister. I did not recognize the person's name, but I am thankful that she kept track of the picture so that I could eventually have it.

I can tell by the way I am dressed in the picture that it was taken when I was on my school's dance team. Our school provided a singing and dancing team to perform at community festivals. I imagine the person with the picture may have also been on the team, and we may have exchanged pictures.

After two years in Kengkok, I returned to Khongsedone Le Collège to finish my secondary schooling. This way I could help care for my siblings at home when Mom was gone to buy and sell out of town. With all the unrest that had been building in our country, my parents felt more comfortable keeping me close.

At my primary school, we had five teachers plus my dad, who was the sixth-grade teacher as well as the principal. Years ago, when my father was a child, any age could attend school, so a first-grade class might have someone twenty-five or even fifty years old there learning to read and write, seated beside the six-year-olds. So when my uncle attended first grade at age fifteen and my dad at age nine, no one thought anything of the age difference. By the time my father was teaching, students were all a similar age within the classroom. Sixth grade was an extremely important school year, and that is why my dad took that grade. Students were continually being reviewed to be sure there were no gaps in their education so that they could be prepared for entrance tests for trade school or whatever career path they wanted to pursue. Dad knew how competitive it was to enter continuing education programs, as it had taken him more than one attempt to get into his field. He was the perfect one to prepare these young minds.

In history we studied periods of our country's historical events as well as information about other countries and their kings, maps, and such topics. We used to have games where we picked a country and tried to find it first on the globe. We were more well-rounded about learning about other countries than kids in the United States are today. Laos was very small and quickly studied, so we moved on to learning about other world areas. We were fascinated by pictures of people with white skin because we had never seen anyone like that before.

Math was just like kids learn here, with classes offered from basic math on up through geometry and algebra.

Science was different at various grade levels. We didn't dissect any animals as an actual class activity, but at home we butchered animals for food, so we would watch and see all the parts of the animal being butchered. Mom would kill and dress chickens almost every week, so we learned the body parts by watching her and eventually learned to butcher on our own. We had fresh fish with heads to cut apart. Any time Mom would buy fish at the market, it would most likely be live, swimming in a bucket. The only way we could purchase fish that had been dressed was to go home and cook it immediately. Mom preferred bringing home live fish to guarantee the freshness. Preparing animals for food forced us to be skilled at dissection, as we cleaned and dressed the fish, chickens, and even frogs we purchased. While children in America were learning about anatomy by dissecting a frog one time in class, my family would dissect an entire bucket of frogs for our evening meal.

In spelling we were drilled because the words were so much harder to spell than English words. Some of the words sound so similar. Americans' ears often cannot pick out the differences. The language is hard to learn; if you don't have the ear for it, you will make mistakes. I often can tell if someone is learning the language because of how they put the little symbol. I can watch someone writing in Laotian and identify almost exactly how much schooling that person had. One example of how difficult the Lao language might be to learn would be to see the similar symbols that have slight variations of accents and pronunciations, yet the meanings of the three would be entirely different:

ມາ **come** (pronounced *ma*)

ມ້າ **soak** (pronounced *mah*, with a little lower pitch)

ມ້າ **horse** (pronounced *maw*, even lower pitched)

Our foreign language was French because our country was a colony of France. Though we began learning letters and words during grade school, we really never did get very good. Teachers would instruct us on the French spelling, English spelling, and the alphabet, at least enough for us to know they used the same alphabet. We always laughed about how they seemed to always be changing things. We had to learn the different endings, like past and present tense, and this was funny to us because we didn't add *-ing* or *-ed* or other endings. Is it any wonder that becoming literate in Laos was challenging? And then to learn French or English—this was even more demanding.

One teacher taught all subjects to first grade up through sixth grade. The teacher would have the only book and wrote everything we needed on the board. We would each have our own notebook and write everything down, which seems tedious today, but it was the only way we knew back then.

After sixth grade, if you were fortunate enough to continue with higher education, text books were available, but they were all in French due to continuing close political relations between Laos and France. Even though we took French every year in grade school, we did not really master the language. We could read the words but not comprehend the meaning. No longer did the teachers write notes on the board in Laotian for us to copy; we depended on the teacher to interpret the French texts for us at this level. We still had to take countless notes and listen carefully. The language was a real barrier at times; even if we knew the content on a test and could have answered perfectly in Laotian, we might still miss the question due to misinterpreting the French words.

Relatives would often send their children to live with us

so that they could attend school. Our house was rather large compared to others, with three divided rooms. If the extra visitors were boys, they were on one side. If they were girls, they would sleep with us kids.

Students walked or rode bicycles to school if they were fortunate to be some of the few who owned bicycles. No matter the weather, kids still walked or biked to school. Our cool season was when it was raining. During winter, it was almost fall-like for a short time, but with many rainy days. We might have to put on a sweater or light jacket during the winter, but the rest of the school year was hot.

Every morning, we would gather outside, line up by grades (boys on one side and girls on the other), face the flag, and recite the pledge to the flag. We would then sing the national anthem. Any announcements would be given, and then we were released to walk in order, first through sixth grades, to go to our classrooms to begin our school time.

Our morning session was from eight o'clock until noon. Then we would walk home for lunch and have recess time, allowing two hours for this. I was fortunate that my dad was a principal, so our house was owned by the school. We lived right next to the school, and I could go home every day. If a student lived more than an hour's walk from the school, that was too far to walk home and back for the afternoon session. The student would have to bring his lunch, which usually consisted of sticky rice, dried fish, jerky, a boiled egg, or whatever the family had on hand. I was always bringing kids home during lunchtime. If I saw someone sitting alone, I would invite them to our house, and they could eat what they brought, or if they did not have anything, they ate with us.

The students who stayed for lunch were very likely to end up dropping out. The distance made their school experience a real hardship for the family. As soon as they could read, they often quit coming. Sometimes my dad would see the potential in these students and wanted to help them. Most likely, he remembered how others reached out to him to help with his education, and he wanted to pay it forward. He would invite them to live at our house to continue their schooling. I only remember boys staying with us. Perhaps the girls' parents didn't feel comfortable sending their daughters to walk that far, or maybe they were needed at home after they learned the basics.

In the afternoon at school we had more classroom time from about two o'clock to four o'clock. Then from four o'clock to five o'clock or so we had recess or perhaps some hands-on time. This is when we would be taught certain life skills. For example, we learned to garden. We had to carry water from the Xe Don River. The only fertilizer we had was manure from hogs or chickens. It really wasn't too far to carry the water, just about a quarter mile or so, but the water was vital to supply in order for the plants to survive. We would save the seeds to plant for the next crop because we didn't have a store to buy seeds. If people gave you seeds once, they would expect you to save your seeds as you harvested. If you didn't save your seeds to use for the next planting, others might not give you any more. You needed to learn to be frugal and wise with your resources. Another skill learned at school that I still use today were the basics of sewing, such as patching a hole in clothes, altering lengths, sewing on buttons, and using different stitches. I also learned to knit and crochet, but that was outside of school. Tutors would teach these additional skills if you could afford the supplies.

I know I was privileged to attend school as a young girl, and I appreciate the role my father played in my early education. As for my part, I always tried to give my best effort at my job as a student. Dad had been a role model for others in his small village when he succeeded in his education. In my dad's eyes, I was the role model here in America. I set the bar high for my siblings and even my youngest uncles and cousins by being the first to complete high school and college. Asians still considered girls to have a greater challenge than boys, so my example was truly inspiring. When any student in the family complained or considered not attending college, Dad would point out how I, even as a girl, was successful here, despite the language barrier. He would not even consider any of us achieving less than four years of college and would prefer we obtained even higher degrees. Education was how Dad determined a person's success, not financial status.

chapter 4

Samia—Peaceful Village Life Disrupted

Samia was a small village located on the east bank of the Xe Don River, a long day's journey on foot from Khongsedone. Rebel forces felt free to travel through the area surrounding Samia and to claim any available supplies from the people there. Even though the country of Laos was officially under French rule, rebel soldiers tended to claim all the towns on the east side of the Xe Don for their own purposes. For years people in and around Samia were accustomed to the rebel soldier foot traffic. Understandably, the locals would have preferred not to deal with this, but we didn't have any choice.

When Mom and Dad were first married, they lived in Samia with Dad's parents in the home Dad had built for them and my two aunts and their families. This house had a lower level with two kitchens, one for each aunt, and a deck on both sides of the house. A huge hallway ran down the center with all the bedrooms located in the front and back of the tin-roofed house. My parents lived there with the extended family until Mom was about to deliver me. Because I was her first child, Mom moved back to Khongsedone to live with her family until I arrived. I was delivered by a doctor in the hospital, and Mom stayed with her parents for her month of recovery, just to be certain all was well.

Grandpa was thrilled with his first grandchild. In fact, he was almost too much help at times. One day while Mom was resting, Grandpa thought he would help out by preparing a bottle for me. He warmed it as he knew he should, but he forgot to let it cool enough for a newborn, and when he fed it to me, he burned my mouth. He also pierced my tiny ears before Mom returned to Samia after her month's stay. Grandpa continued to dote on me all my life. With a new baby, though, my parents felt they needed their own space, so Mom and Dad purchased some land and built a home for us near the school.

Ott, Sing, and Tay were born at home in Samia, with Dad leading in each of their deliveries, assisted by a midwife. Apparently my parents were more accomplished birthing experts by that time. I remember when I was a little girl waking up to a commotion in the house ... Mom was giving birth! I was so excited because many people would be coming to visit. We would enjoy great food, and everyone would be playing games and visiting into the night. Friends and family kept visiting for weeks after the baby arrived, helping take care of the household while Mom recovered. Ott and I were talking one day about how we did not celebrate birthdays when we were growing up and how some Laotians did not even know their actual birthdays. He chuckled when he said that our people celebrated in grand style when we came into the world and again when we left it. All the years in between birth and death did not require too much fanfare.

Living in Samia was a huge adjustment for Mom, who came from the city environment of Khongsedone to a small rice farming community. She was used to having a farmers' market to purchase food every morning, running water, and even a few hours of electricity each evening. It was definitely a change to have to hunt, fish, and farm for their food.

My dad fished daily in the Xe Don River. One of the techniques he used was every evening when we were at the river for gardening or bathing, Dad would set out his net across the river. Then early the next morning he would gather the net to bring back to the house. Hopefully, there would be enough fish stuck in the net for breakfast and lunch. Dad was constantly repairing his net because big fish would often break through, leaving a hole behind. Another technique he used was for times when the river's current was strong enough that the net wouldn't hold up. He would place several baited hooks on one longer line and stretch that across the river to the other side, spacing the hooks carefully so they did not get tangled.

In addition to fishing, my dad also hunted anything he could find, such as birds, lizards, and other small game. Mom learned to raise some chickens, ducks, and a few pigs to supplement Dad's fishing and hunting. Occasionally someone in the community might have extra food to sell from butchering cattle, water buffalo, or a hog. She always purchased from the local people whenever she could. When a neighbor wanted to butcher livestock, he would usually ask another neighbor to help pay on the animal, but often, people didn't have money to spare. This was not the case with my mom; she always had money on hand for food. With a large family to feed, she was nearly always willing to go in on the butchered animal. She would share with my dad's family and then make jerky for the little ones to enjoy after that. Of course, we did not have an official dehydrator due to no available electricity. Instead, on a sunny day, Mom would spread out the pieces of meat on bamboo trays and cover it all with an insect netting frame, similar to an umbrella, but the sun could still get through to dry out the meat. If it were a rainy day, we still had a way to make jerky. Our kitchen was a few steps from the main house, and it was open on the sides, with a roof to protect us from the rain. Mom would cook on an open fire there, and Dad fixed a loosely woven tray for the meat to hang over the fire. The smoke and heat would dry the meat and keep the bugs away.

Not only did Mom purchase from the locals, but she also saw an opportunity to use her sharp trading skills and her talented seamstress skills to provide badly needed food, clothing, and other supplies to Samia and nearby towns. Even though no one had much money, they could barter with Mom. Perhaps a beautiful dress to wear to the upcoming temple festival might be traded for an IOU stating that a portion of next year's rice crop be sent to her for payment.

Mom eventually began traveling back to her hometown to get supplies as well as items to sell back in Samia. The several-mile journey back to Khongsedone was not an easy trip. When they were dating, Dad used to take a moped (a small motorized vehicle barely powerful enough to carry his weight) on the dirt trail from Samia to see Mom. He also had to travel this route to pick up his salary for teaching. No one used the banks, and no credit cards or checks were used, only cash.

When Mom began to bring items to resell, rather than navigate the small, rough dirt trails, she would hire a fishing boat to take her and bring her back on the Xe Don River. Mom had to reserve her travel date in advance by sending word with another traveler to let him know she wanted to go. I remember joining her on these trips when I was quite young. The boat had a cover to keep the sun off us, but if it rained, we still got wet. It would take us days to travel back to see our grandparents, get the goods, and return home with the loaded boat. We could only travel when the water was high enough for the boat to pass the sandbars and rocks. If we had some type of emergency and had to travel in times of low water, we had to have some men folk along to carry the boat over the rocks and debris. We walked along the bank, while they carried the boat through the rough spots.

These trips sometimes gave us the opportunity to meet new people and enjoy Laotian hospitality. If the boat's motor broke down, we might be stranded in a small village along the way, perhaps even overnight. We would sometimes be welcomed to a home of an acquaintance of a friend or sometimes even invited to stay with strangers. The Laotian way was to provide lodging and meals to anyone in need. This helped Mom build a network of friends who were also welcome to stay in our home any time they were passing through Samia. After Mom's reputation as a seamstress grew, we often had customers from neighboring villages show up at our house to have Mom custom design a beautiful garment for the lady of the house for the next festival or even for a daughter's wedding. We always offered them a meal or even lodging for the night if it was too far for them to return home in the same day. Our area did not have hotels of any kind; we simply depended on each other's hospitality if we chose to travel away from our own village.

At the time, no one really knew how successful my mom's merchandising business was, no—even my dad. She had such a great sense of what the people needed. For example, when it was almost time for farmers to plant, she would load extra straw hats to keep the sun off them and new plowshares the farmers might need for their water buffalo to pull through the earth. She might plan ahead three months or more by purchasing beautiful cloth that ladies might want her to sew into a dress for an upcoming festival. She had a definite instinct to make money.

Dad was busy at his work and didn't realize how many transactions she made at home. She took cash to purchase the goods, and any cash left over was used to purchase gold. In fact, she often carried gold with her, but no one saw it. Her seamstress skills were handy to sew hidden seams or pockets to stash some small gold items. Because we didn't use a bank, she had to find a good hiding place for her cash. Sometimes the best hiding places were in plain sight; the baby's pillow often held the cash she had on hand, and no one knew that—not even Dad.

Though it was a small village without many luxuries, we were very fortunate to benefit from a medical clinic in Samia. The clinic treated military personnel located in the camp there, as well as all the locals. Staff members would come to the home for a house call if the patient was too sick or old to travel to the clinic. These caring employees were on call 24/7. Malaria was a deadly disease that swept through many villages, causing many deaths. Our family knew the pain malaria caused firsthand, losing my mom's thirteen-year-old sister, ຄຳ ມ (Kim), when I was in first grade. When the clinic opened, they were able to treat the high fever accompanying malaria, and they saved the lives of many children. The clinic provided medicine that was unavailable to most people at the time, including treatment for my dad's asthma. All clinic and hospital employees were paid by the government, and all services and medicines were given at no charge to the patient.

A male nurse practitioner named Thongdam was in charge at the clinic, assisted by a few nurses, and they could easily take care of the people in the area. However, when the Laotian government sent troops into the Samia area, their patient load increased dramatically. The staff could not adequately serve the military along with the villagers. They needed help, and they received it in the form of Bouabane, a male army nurse recently assigned by the government to the hospital in Khongsedone. While previously serving for a few years alongside American troops, Bouabane had learned valuable medical knowledge and skills. The Khongsedone hospital staff realized that Bouabane's skills would be much more valuable to the overwhelmed Samia clinic, so they sent him there. Bouabane taught malaria prevention to the locals, training them to use mosquito nets and boil the any water used for human consumption. He also educated them about the importance of washing out the drinking water pots every day and keeping the pots covered to prevent mosquitos from laying eggs in their water source. Eventually, he took on more of the leadership role at the clinic.

Samia had no rentals or hotels to lodge the clinic's newest asset, so Thongdam took Bouabane under his wing, finding a place for him to live. Thongdam's relatives agreed to house Bouabane, and this is where Bouabane met his future wife. Bouabane married Bounnao, Thongdam's niece. Bouabane and Bounnao became our family's longtime friends. He eventually passed away in 2018, and I attended his funeral in Elgin, Illinois.

Although my parents were doing well financially and thriving in Samia, they were not without stress, even when the school was established and doing well. A group of rebels who broke away from the Laotian government began to solicit my dad to join them. He did not accept their request, so they began to escalate their efforts by showing up at night, looking for him, and forcing him to go with them. A couple of times he was taken away to go with them to their hideout in the woods in a hidden cave. These rebels realized how valuable my dad could be to their forces. They needed someone with an education who would be an effective leader, and they felt Dad was a perfect candidate. If he would agree to join their forces, he would have been a huge asset. However, he did not share their beliefs, and he would not leave his family, so he resisted their efforts to convert him. There was no real way for us to know where the rebels had taken Dad. However, some of the townspeople followed the trail, caught up with them, and somehow got them to release Dad to come back to run the school. After these incidents, people in town would run to Dad to tell him to take cover if they heard any stirrings about rebel soldiers coming to Samia to get him. Dad would take off and hide, sometimes in a ditch or anywhere they couldn't see him. He sometimes even swam across the river to the other side to avoid capture. This was not only stressful for Dad but was just as stressful for Mom. Rebel soldiers would come to the house and demand that she tell them where he was, but she was thankful that she didn't know and could not give him up. Dad just took off. The fears and nightmares of worrying about when they would show up next and whether they would take Dad away, leaving her with all those kids to protect, made her life miserable.

As the Laotian government learned of my dad's harassment from the rebel party, they felt obligated to protect him and his thriving school, that was providing better education for the area. As a result, they moved a military camp right next to the school to protect the area. This influx of soldiers was the reason Bouabane was sent to the Samia clinic. Because we lived next to the school, we also were next to this military base. You might think this made our family more secure, but instead, it made my mom even more fearful. If any confrontation between the two parties would start up, our home would be right in the middle of it all. It was common knowledge that the rebels were very sneaky fighters who were anything but fair. Every night the army base sent troops out to patrol different areas known for foot traffic. During daytime, they were back at the headquarters near the school, and then the next night they would be out again at different spots, looking for invaders. Some townspeople volunteered to be trained and armed to help guard Samia and watch for rebel intruders. At one point, there was a shootout where we lost some village men, and this heightened my mom's fear for my dad's safety as well as ours.

Mom began to seek a new place for us to live, even though Dad had not yet agreed to go. He was not ready to give up on his hometown and his dream to build the school system there. However, Dad's reluctance did not deter Mom from pursuing a safer place for her family. Mom would travel to Khongsedone for her business, and that was also where Dad's boss lived. She would share with his boss about the unrest in Samia and her fear for our family's safety, asking for Dad to be transferred somewhere safer. Still, no transfer happened. In the meanwhile, Mom was making lots of money and had no real place to spend it, but that problem was eventually solved.

On one of their trips to Khongsedone, they passed by an empty lot for sale on the outskirts of the city. This would be perfect for my dad, who enjoyed more space than the middle of the city would have offered. My mom immediately wanted to build a house there, but my dad hesitated, assuming it would cost far too much for them. He did not realize just how profitable Mom's business had become. Imagine my dad's surprise when Mom presented him with a baby pillow full of money—enough to pay for the land as well as for the new home construction! Without banks, everything was paid in cash up front, requiring a down payment to start and payments to continue as it was built. They were able to fund their new home through Mom's stash she had accumulated. Grandpa Song oversaw the building project when she was not there.

Actually, Mom's saving skills provided more than just a place to live; they also saved the life of child number two. Her savings at the time Sing was born would have been enough for a new home, but he was very sick and required lots of medical payments. What a blessing that she had the money available for him! There was no insurance, and all treatments required cash payment. As a result, the new home had to wait until Mom replaced her stash. After child number four (Tay) was born, Mom's cash in the pillow had been replenished, and construction could move forward.

Finally, construction on our new house was completed and ready for residents. Yet, we were not going to be the first ones to occupy our new home. After a few more years of stress and the additional responsibility of protecting and caring for four kids, my dad finally got frightened enough to agree to move, but the job opening for Dad's work was not in Khongsedone. Instead it was in Khamthong. We were not able to relocate to Khongsedone until a few years later. In the meanwhile, my parents rented the house out to some high-ranking army officers because it was close to the army camp and was nicer than most other homes in the area.

The clinic and the school each served the community for several years, but eventually the climate in Samia became progressively more unsettling. Rebel soldiers repeatedly tried to recruit workers they deemed valuable to the resistance, escalating their pressure more as time went on. Each time the rebels came into the village, they would demand all the supplies that the school and the clinic had on hand. Government workers in Samia grew more and more fearful, and they began to leave the area. After we left Samia, the clinic closed, and the school my dad loved so much began to lose key teachers, eventually ceasing to function as a school. This was so sad for everyone in the community.

Even though we had left the area, my parents were still able to empower young people from Samia who wanted to continue their schooling, inviting them to live at our house in Khamthong to go to school. Our home became sort of like a foster home to kids who wanted an opportunity to better their lives through education. We fed and clothed these kids just like they were part of the family. This was a chance for our family to pay forward the blessing of education that Dad had received.

Eventually, the rebel forces' actions opened the door for the

Communist party to take control of our Laotian government. Several changes occurred, including reopening the school in Samia. Even though the school opened once more, it did not really function well. The new government did not have a budget to pay teachers, so the school system was once again struggling and losing good teachers. Another reason for the teacher shortage was that so many had fled to Thailand, to lead a safer, more secure life in the refugee camps there. Thailand was also a third world country with widespread poverty and other problems of their own, but they were gracious enough to allow the refugees to stay there temporarily until they could arrange to legally immigrate to another country. Even today, Samia struggles to appropriately fund education.

chapter 5

Khamthong—New Ventures

Around 1966 or 1967, my dad was transferred to oversee another school system, and we moved to Khamthong, which was considered to be a safer area than Samia. However, it was difficult to leave behind Dad's home village, my parents' home for the first few years of their marriage. It was especially hard on my dad's mother, CƲ ᷂ (Peu). Our moving van was a boat that took us down the Xe Don. I can still picture my devastated grandma Peu sitting on the bank of the river, watching us float away. Even though I was young, this made an impression on me. She was so broken and distraught. After that, she became very ill, and we almost lost her before she eventually recovered. Such deep grief and hopelessness can cause a physical illness, and a few years later, I would experience this for myself.

The city of Khamthong was on Route 13, the well-traveled main road running from the capital of Vientiane in northern Laos to Pakse, another large city in the southern part of Laos. Khongsedone, where Mom grew up, was only about ten miles north of Khamthong, so Mom was much closer to her family now. At this time, we had four children in the family, and I was just about to begin school in first grade. With a much better road than we had in Samia, my mom's journeys to get supplies in

Khongsedone were far easier, and we also felt much safer living farther from most of the rebel forces' activity.

Because our new home was located west of the Xe Don River, we would be farther from the Ho Chi Minh Trail than when we lived in Samia. The Ho Chi Minh Trail was an area of mountain and jungle trails and paths running north and south in eastern Laos. North Vietnam used the trail to send troops and supplies into South Vietnam, Cambodia, and Laos during these violent years of the Vietnam War. Military troops set explosives and bombed the area in an attempt to prevent Communist travel, and the violence spilled out into the surrounding Lao region. Rebel soldiers felt free to come and go through this area and did so regularly. We were thankful to relocate farther from all of this activity.

Our housing in Khamthong was rather luxurious compared to other hutches and small homes in the community. We lived in a strong, well-built concrete house that I believe had once been a post office. When we first moved there, this was a two-family dwelling. One side had a teacher who had served as the school leader, even though he was not certified to be a principal. He had a family with four or five children. My family with our four kids moved into the other side. Each side had two big, open rooms, with our side having the larger space. We set up our beds. Each bed Dad built had a canopy frame, and Mom custom made mosquito netting to fit the frame. The girls' bed was large enough to hold me and my cousin who nannied us, as well as another visitor or two if needed. The boys' beds were like mine, lined up in the same room. We hung up privacy curtains around my parents' bed in the main living area, and we were set. I guess you could say we had the open-floor-plan design that is so popular on home improvement television shows now, even though we didn't know about the concept at the time. Another building came with the property, originally serving as two kitchens, one for each family.

After we lived there about a year, the other family was transferred so that the teacher could lead another school district. Then the second building's role changed somewhat. One side of the building was still a kitchen, but the other side was set up as extra space for lodging in case we ran out of room in the main house. The empty side of the main house was used to lodge student teachers who were eager to learn teaching skills from my dad. By this time, Pakse offered teaching programs. The people who ran the Pakse school knew my dad and that he received his training from Vientiane, which was the elite school. Students who studied under Dad had a high success rate of passing the entrance exams to continue their education, so future teachers wanted to come to Dad's school to learn from him.

We also hosted students from my dad's hometown of Samia. The people there wanted their children to learn from him. These students were usually a little older and often needing to take a refresher course to pass the entrance exams for further education. Dad might just let them sit in the classroom to review the materials they need help with.

Our guests had some flexible schedules and living arrangements. Some of the older students who lived farther away had an open invitation and could stay at a moment's notice, perhaps because of bad weather or any other issue that would require them to stay in town rather than miss a day of school. These kids sometimes brought their own food, but if they did not have anything, they ate with us. They might go fishing with my dad and learn various other life skills. He cared for them beyond the classroom. We would never know how many bodies might be under our roof for the night, but we didn't care. As long as we had mosquito netting available, all overnight guests were welcome.

In addition to the two main rooms in the second building, we also had an odd little room that had no purpose we could see, but we put it to good use anyway. The little room became the spot for the chickens to gather to roost at night and also where they laid their eggs. Laotian custom was to keep free-range chickens for food, but we kids named our chickens and kept them as pets. This made it very hard for Mom to butcher them; one kid would be devastated if his chicken became dinner. If Mom wanted to serve chicken, she would have to be very sneaky and slip in when the kids weren't around to snag one for butchering. Once the chicken was dressed and ready to cook, no one could identify whose pet was sacrificed for the meal, and all was fine. We kept a few ducks as well. Although we would have loved to enjoy roasted duck now and then, we resisted the temptation and instead kept them for their eggs, which we ate for breakfast most days because we let our chickens hatch their eggs for baby chicks. We had no refrigeration, but eggs were fine to keep at room temperature if they were not washed. Eggs have a natural protective bloom on them to keep bacteria out of the fresh egg. In America, eggs are washed before they reach the consumer, so they must be refrigerated. We also owned some pigs that were allowed free-range roaming around our yard.

Mom had a large garden area on the riverbank area of our property, and we had to put bamboo fencing up to keep the roaming animals out. Anyone who was staying with us would help with the garden and benefit from the delicious produce. Visitors also gathered firewood. I recall one technique they used to gather a large amount of wood in a short time. During the monsoon season, the river was flooded to the point that the swollen waters washed out dead trees and limbs on the banks. This dry wood floated as it traveled down the river. The young people staying with us would go out on the river in canoes and catch the wood as it floated by and drag each piece to the bank, creating a big pile. Later on, they could come to the pile and chop up the pieces with a machete to be hauled to the house for firewood.

Dad continued fishing daily in Khamthong as he did in Samia. I remember how he caught fish when the river was flooded. Two of the young people who stayed with us would set out on the river in the canoe. One would paddle, and the other would stand with a framed net held out in front of the canoe. When the net was brought up, they would find tiny fish and shrimp that we only saw during flood stage.

The small community of Khamthong provided my first chance to try my own skills as a salesperson. When Dad would have a good catch of fish—more than my family could use for that day—my mom told me I could try to sell the extra fish in the neighborhood and keep the money. That was a great motivator for me. Mom would string the fish together, and then I put them on a tray and began to go door to door to see who would like to purchase them. Mom gave me a good idea what to charge based on what she usually paid for fish. Early on, I was so young that I made a few mistakes along the way. For example, I did not have a pouch or anything to put my money in, and so I placed the money on the fish tray and carried the tray on the top of my head. When I got home, I didn't have much left on the tray; it had all blown away. What a lesson that was ... All that work and successful sales gone with the wind. After that, I was a little more careful. At the start, I didn't know how to count or make change, so my customers usually took care of it themselves. I hope they were honest! I saved up my money until I had a chance to buy some candy.

Khamthong is where I started school, and three more siblings were born here. Here, my dad became even more influential and was often sought for advice for various activities, even beyond running the school. For instance, when the village would have a fundraising festival for the temple, rather important wealthy people from nearby cities would come to our village to offer support, largely due to my dad's influence. All around the school, Dad had cleaned up the area and added benches and parklike facilities where community members could gather for picnics and other events. People appreciated the improvements, and this was also a reflection of Dad's influence in town. He used the area improvements as a teaching opportunity for the students, who learned how to landscape as well as how to care for their environment. When Dad's supervisors would come for an inspection, the school would host a big gathering in the beautiful park area, which was a chance for my dad and his students to showcase their hard work.

With the improved school grounds available for events, Dad's school began to host an annual fundraising festival to provide additional money for upkeep of the school and schoolyard. This festival was an exciting time for all the students and the community. We were trained how to perform traditional Laotian dances. Students with gifted voices practiced and practiced in order to showcase their talents. The teachers worked with the students for months to prepare for the big day. Because the students all worked hard to prepare, the community all felt ownership of the beautification of the school and its grounds. The community took pride in how everyone had worked together and how so many came from out of the area to help support this thriving school. The students were so very proud of their extended family and friends coming from out of town to see even the smallest children perform. Most traditional festivals included a Lao Lamvong dance to help raise funds. This was when either a famous band or a local band would provide music for dancing, and community members would pay to have them play their favorite songs, and also they could pay to choose their dance partner. It was a time to dress up and enjoy the fun. Our school benefited greatly from the money raised at our annual festival's dance. All the money raised could be used for whatever my dad felt would benefit the students. He might purchase text books, awards for hard-working students, pens, pencils, or notebooks. The money might also pay for food to provide for the festival, whether it was a water buffalo, cow, hog, or any other larger animal. More people came if food was provided, so this worked to our benefit.

During this time in Khamthong, I was old enough to learn of another Laotian tradition—the joy of childbirth and all the rituals and activities surrounding this blessed time. In our village, we had no doctors or hospitals, so all births were in the home with a midwife assisting the father. When the new baby arrived, rather than giving the parents space and quiet time to recuperate, our community people would all gather at the home of the new baby. Some people brought food, and others came to eat and celebrate. Everyone visited, played games, and enjoyed the happy time. This would go on day and night for at least a week. An open fire was built inside the house. They would build a ring of banana tree trunks and fill it with a dirt base under the fire to protect the floor. The new mother would stay by the fire in a newly built bamboo bed as long as she could stand it. Young, able-bodied neighbors would volunteer to fetch water from the river to store in a container at the house to be available any time the new mother would like to take a bath. The new mom was also encouraged to drink plenty of hot water, always boiled adequately to make it safe. The young people also gathered firewood to have plenty on hand for the continual fire. During this time, young single girls often came to assist the family with cooking, cleaning, and childcare for the family. This provided opportunity for young men in the area to come see these eligible young ladies in an appropriate setting.

They would often play fun card games or homemade games, as long as the new mother's needs were provided by the attending visitors. Late at night, the little children of the house were asleep, and the elderly had gone home, so the young people were left to tend to the new mother's needs. They didn't want the fire to die out, but it should not be too hot either, so the young people rotated in and out on the responsibilities there. At this time, they could socialize with each other, and they would often cook something delicious like a big pot of chicken and rice soup or hot and spicy papaya salad to keep them awake and to be alert companions to the new mother. Some families did not have money to provide food for everyone, so the community would see to it that supplies were available for those attending. I remember my dad had a big kerosene lantern he would loan out for his contribution for the family, and sometimes he would also provide the kerosene if they could not afford to buy their own. When the new mother finally felt healed enough to not need assistance, she would stop sitting by the fire and transition into her regular bed to rest for the remainder of her recuperation time, which usually was about a month. The tending community members would then go home.

In current times, and especially in the United States, families are much smaller. Families in Laos when I was growing up had several children spanning several years. We had no methods of birth control, so women continued having children until menopause. It was very common to have aunts and uncles who were your own age or even younger. Grandma Houay's three youngest children were close to the age of me and my next two siblings. As a matter of fact, my youngest uncle, Khamla, was almost the same age as my brother Ott. When Khamla was born, my grandma was very sick and could not care for my baby uncle. Family members met to decide who would care for the new baby, with the sad thought that my grandma might not live to raise him. Grandpa Song's older brother, the one responsible for bringing Grandpa Song from China to Laos, had only one son and desperately wanted to raise another son. My parents really did not want to give him away, so they needed a good excuse. Mom had the perfect solution. At that time in Asia, we did not have any kind of baby formula available, so if the mother could not care for the baby and no wet nurse was available, the only option was canned condensed milk, and often babies did not thrive on this. Not only did this milk lack necessary nutrition, but one can would last a newborn a few days. Without refrigeration, the milk's quality was questionable. Babies who consumed the canned milk would usually have stomach issues, and the baby's health would suffer. Because my mom was nursing Ott, she could easily take Khamla as well. My great-uncle's family did not have access to a wet nurse, so Khamla came to stay with us.

Thankfully, Grandma recovered and was able to take Khamla back after about a year, when he was weaned. Eventually, this baby uncle became my grandparents' caregiver. They lived with Khamla as long as they were alive, and Grandma lived to be ninety-seven years old! The only time Uncle Khamla did not live with his parents was in the first year of his life when he lived with us. I remember Uncle Khamla questioning who his biological parents really were. This probably came from his older brother planting doubt in his mind. When they got in arguments like all siblings do, he would tell Khamla he did not belong to their parents; he was adopted. Eventually, we had to reassure Khamla that he really belonged to my grandparents, telling him the story of how he survived his first year.

When we moved to Khamthong, my mom began to work as a seamstress. Because of her reputation, she had plenty of business, usually running a month or two behind. However, she could not keep sewing full time due to some health issues. At this point, she still had some items to sell and some products she brought with her. She continued to make money, but not as much as before in Samia. There were more stores here to provide goods, so Mom's previous buy-and-sell business was not as essential to the community and therefore was not as profitable. She had to find a new way to make money, and this led to her next entrepreneurial adventure.

Mom sold some of her gold to purchase a taxi. Asian taxis at that time ran a little differently than we are accustomed to today in America. A taxi might be as small as a tuk tuk (a motorized rickshaw), or it could be a car, truck, van, or even a large cargo truck. Any vehicle could be used. City taxi services were located in stations called hubs. A taxi served more as a bus service, transporting people from town to town rather than just a few blocks away within the city limit. If you lived in a small village and wanted to use a taxi for travel, you would walk to the main road and flag down a passing taxi. If they had room, they would pick you up, and if they did not have room, you had to wait for the next one. People would pack in like sardines in order to catch their ride; they could not be sure when the next taxi might come that way again. Once you were aboard, you would need to warn the driver when your stop was near so that you could get out. Some would have a little bell to ring to catch the driver's attention. When you arrived at your destination, the driver would tell you the fee, you would pay it, and then you would go on your way. When you were ready to return home, you would try to catch a taxi going back toward your home, and you would have to go through the process again.

Mom's vehicle was a pickup truck that she converted into a taxi by adding metal framework over the bed to create an upper level. People packed into both levels for their journey. She usually reserved the cab of the taxi for herself. One exception would be if a monk traveled with her. Out of respect, she would allow him to sit in the cab; a monk would never sit close to a woman, so she was at ease with him joining her up front. When Mom began her service, she would be gone by early morning and would stay out all day, traveling back and forth usually between Khongsedone and Pakse and the communities between. We would never know where she was or when she was coming home. We had no cell phones back then, of course. We had no ambulance services, so sometimes a taxi was contracted to serve as an ambulance. In that case, the family of the patient would pay a price comparable to what Mom would have received with all her customers getting on and off at various stops on that particular route in order to drive the patient straight to a hospital. Each trip would start at a taxi hub, or station, and the driver was responsible for finding customers who were ready to leave when the taxi was ready to depart. Rounding up riders was an important part of Mom's day. Each trip's profit depended on how many riders she picked up. The more customers, the better.

Looking back now, I feel this may not have been one of her best ventures. Because she was out of the house running her taxi service, the kids were left at home with the nanny, and Mom was not there to oversee the day-to-day activities. In the past, both Mom and Dad were at home every day. Sure, we had always had a nanny to help with the kids, but Mom was there nearly all the time, cooking and helping watch over us. Even though we were not in danger and nothing bad really happened then, I learned what it was like to have both parents working outside of the home. Some days were hard, and Mom was not in the best mood when she returned, so we lost even more of our quality time with our mom. Because of this, I decided I would be a stay-at-home mom while my children were young. I knew how comforting it was to have my mother available during my early years.

Even though I was not thrilled with Mom's taxi venture, I do have some very happy memories of that taxi. Sometimes in the evening, Mom and Dad would take the taxi to Khongsedone to visit family, and we would all pile in and enjoy the experience. We were often treated to snacks like ice cream or cool, refreshing drinks with ice, delights that were only offered in the city. Sometimes we even enjoyed an Asian noodle meal prepared in the city rather than in Mom's kitchen. Riding in Mom's truck taxi to the city certainly beat taking the boat taxi from Samia to Khongsedone as we used to do. The previous all-day adventure to the grandparents now was a quick thirty-minute trip. Another benefit of the taxi service was that we had a better variety of food that Mom brought home from the big city on her taxi runs. We weren't as dependent on the catch of the day or a neighbor's butchering habits. In fact, one Vietnamese gentleman neighbor was an excellent butcher and whole-hog roaster. Every once in a while, my parents would buy a hog for him to prepare, and we would enjoy a hog roast. Often we would plan a roast for the times my dad's supervisors would be visiting, which offered a fine experience for the visitors.

Summers in Khamthong offered a bit of a change in our friends and playmates. During the school year, I had some very close friends to hang out with, and many of these traveled to the village to attend school. When summer came, these close friends were not in town, so I tended to hang out with others. Some of them might not even attend school, but we certainly found ways to have fun during the summer months. These were the years of unstructured play time. We might go together to find some trees with ripened fruit to pick and eat, or perhaps hunt for berries. Usually we would go as a group to play or explore. We had so much freedom as small children in the village; nobody would harm us, and life was safe and fun.

One sad memory of living in Khamthong happened when we returned to school the start of my third-grade year. One of my best friends did not return to join us for school. We eventually learned that she had contracted malaria and had died. That was a very hard time for me and my friends. Babies often did not survive in our area, and one time my friend's mother died giving birth to a baby, but this was the first time that I lost someone I actually knew as a friend.

chapter 6

Khongsedone—A War Zone Intensifies

We lived in Khamthong until the end of my fourth-grade year, around 1970, when Dad accepted a promotion to an assistant superintendent of schools in Mom's dream location, her hometown of Khongsedone. This was quite an opportunity that he could not pass up, even though it meant he would have to adjust to city living rather than the rural life he was accustomed to. No longer would he be able to hunt, fish, and grow food for the family. We would have to pay for all we ate, and this took much more money than we needed in Samia. All of our lifestyles had to change. Mom's opportunity to make money through buying and selling was no longer available. Mom and Dad's circle of friends began to include school leaders, politicians, and other notable city figures. In the small village, we kids were used to having the freedom of running unmonitored from home to home, but in the city, we were much more restricted. We had to undergo the stress of moving and then try to make new friends in a new school. City people were not as friendly as people I'd known before. I noticed more cliques and kids whispering behind others' backs. It just wasn't what I was used to. Dad was gone from the home more often now, going to other schools to inspect them and instruct them. My parents seemed to be busier with their own circles and obligations and had less time for us kids than they used to have.

Another change for us was our school experience. Four of us were in school, and we had to walk almost two miles each way to our grade school, which was much different from when we lived right the beside the school. The city had more traffic we had to deal with, and we were not used to city street safety rules. The school was much bigger, and we sort of fell through the cracks. No longer were we known as the principal's kids; we were just faces in the crowd. The academic subjects were overall the same, but this system was just so much bigger and more impersonal.

However, one bright spot was that we finally got to move into my mom's dream home that Mom and Dad had built while we were living in Samia. As much as it had been my mom's dream to live in this house, her joy was overshadowed by the growing war activity. The escalating Vietnam War brought turmoil to our area. Our family's safety was compromised, especially Dad's. Dad worked as a teacher for the government, which was under French rule. Teachers, soldiers, nurses, and policemen all got paid from this French-ruled government, which was in opposition to the rebels in the Lao Issara party.

During my fifth-grade year, Khongsedone, even though it was located on the supposed safe side of the Xe Don River, became a civil war zone. The division in the country began on a small scale, with the leading Lao rulers splitting on their loyalties. The new movement was called the Lao Issara, which was an anticolonial armed nationalist movement of rebels who wanted to be independent from the French government. The Lao Issara gathered in strength for several years, especially when the current (French) government threatened and even killed key leaders and politicians who did not support the government. Those feeling threatened were compelled to leave, fleeing for their lives. The only available option was to join the Lao Issara, who were hiding in woods and caves, training and building their forces. The Lao Issara were looking to claim more and more land for their territory. They succeeded, gaining village after village and city after city on their side of the river. For the most part, the French-run government allowed this to happen, realizing that openly fighting the rebels' efforts would cause great harm to the general population. Issara soldiers were not nearly as concerned about civilians; Issara troops fought ruthlessly, burning bridges, planting land mines, and even using civilian areas to hide out, shielding them from the government military.

The French-run government may have overlooked Issara taking over small communities and villages, but Khongsedone was a different story because of its location near Route 13, the only supply route from Vientiane to Pakse and other southern cities. The entire country depended on produce from the south, and the country would be cut in half if they lost Khongsedone. The Lao Issara wanted to claim Khongsedone so that they could disrupt supplies and travel from north to south, causing major problems for the French-run government military as well as for all citizens. The government would not sit back and allow this to happen without a fight. Both Issara and the French government were willing to fight for control of Khongsedone.

During the day, things seemed pretty much normal. However, nighttime was a different story. Khongsedone was a few miles from Route 13 with one main road from the highway to the city. Our home was situated directly on this road, within sight of the government army camp. Mom and Dad selected this location for their home years before because it was on the outskirts of the city. Dad wanted to have more space rather than moving into the crowded city center. However, living so close to the military camp endangered us more than we could have imagined.

When the camp was under threat of attack, we received a warning to take cover. We might get the warning by word of mouth, or sometimes helicopters would drop flyers down on the area. Mom would usually take us to my grandparents' home in the city or to the homes of other friends or family. The main road into Khongsedone was the only paved street in the city, with businesses lining each side of the downtown area. My grandparents' storefront home was there in the downtown area, along the paved street. I also remember sometimes simply heading to a big concrete tube running under the road near our house to avoid stray bullets rather than taking the time and effort to flee into the city. These warnings seemed to happen so frequently that we sometimes did not leave, and at times, we did not even take cover. I guess we let our guard down.

I clearly recall one time when we decided to stay in our own home, even after a warning. In the middle of the night, our family was awakened by loud explosions. Mom and Dad woke us up. All of us were upstairs, and the only way down was the outside staircase. As we were scrambling down those outside stairs, I saw a missile head streak past our house and land at the entrance of the army camp, dropping in a billowing explosion, no more than a quarter mile away. This incident was a turning point for us. We had to find alternate living arrangements. My parents rented a property next door to my grandparents' home to sleep at night. We would come back home and carry on with our regular activities during the day and then return to our rented place at night. Once again, I was thankful for my mom's taxi that could quickly and easily transport us between our day and night homes rather than having to walk. Mom was also comforted to be near her parents in case my dad got called in to serve in the army reserves. We lived in fear like this, unsettled and always on edge, for close to a year. Most of the time we attended school, but after a bombing or a scare of that sort, my parents sometimes kept us home, and at other times, school would be cancelled because the teacher would be called for military duty.

Looking back at this time, I can say that my fifth-grade school year was nothing short of a nightmare. Between the new, large city setting, my mom working outside the home, bombing scares on a regular basis, intermittent school attendance, and my dad serving in the reserves away from home at night, my once secure family structure was crumbling. I am so thankful for my grandparents and aunts and uncles who were there for my mom and all of us kids. Our family functioned day-to-day, living in fear and living on edge.

Before I finished fifth grade, things got even worse. I knew very little about the Lao government at that time. I knew that my dad worked for the government. I knew that teachers, nurses, doctors, and policemen all got paid by the government. Anybody who got paid by the government could be called in to carry a gun to fight. When my dad got called in to fight along with the army, I realized he was more than a teacher or principal. His administration skills and reputation placed him at a higher risk to the Issara because they feared he would lead people to retaliate against the newly formed regime. This placed my dad on the list of known enemies of the Lao Issara party. He was now a soldier, put in harm's way by the government.

Lao Issara soldiers regularly crossed the Xe Don River, heading toward Khongsedone, creeping into the outer city limits at night. They were sneaky, at times walking into the city unarmed, never wearing any type of uniform, scouting our people, buying goods, and studying the pattern of the government military. It was impossible for the French government troops to know when they were being scouted because even though theses intruders were spies, they were Lao citizens who looked and acted just like the locals. They began planting themselves in the city without our knowledge. No one could know exactly when they came into the area; maybe they had been there for months. We received warning after warning that Issara could be about to invade the city, and one morning the warning became a reality.

Every morning, we had a routine at our nighttime lodging in the downtown area. Without electricity for refrigeration, Mom had to go to the market to shop for our day's food items. The market area had shops and stands with various types of foods and other items from residents within the city as well as from local farmers and gardeners who came into the city to sell their goods. These out-of-town vendors would then buy supplies with their profits before heading out of the city. In order to have the best selection, Mom always left very early, before we got up. While she was marketing, we would eventually get up and begin getting ready for school before she returned with her purchases for the day.

On May 17, 1971, Mom was at morning market, but instead of finding bustling, busy stands, she found what was essentially a ghost town. The usual vendors from outside the city limits did not come, and word of mouth spread that this was because the outer city limits were full of Issara soldiers. Mom came home panicking with the news, and Dad did not come home at all from his nightly military watch. Instead of our normal routine of Mom leisurely shopping at the market and then the kids waking up and getting ready for school, we were frantically throwing our goods together to leave as soon as we could.

We did not dare go back to our daytime home where we could have grabbed more of our belongings. The danger was far too great to travel so near to the army camp. We had to make do with the few items we had with us at our night quarters near my grandparents. We had no phone and no electronics at all, so I do not know if Mom had a chance to send to word to Dad that we were leaving or which way we would go. She could have asked someone to relay a message, but she did not really know exactly where we were headed. I know they were each doing their duty—Mom keeping us safe, and Dad serving in active duty rather than his usual reserve duty to help push back the Issara soldiers in the area.

The city population was in a panic, realizing that our city was in the center of a violent war between the Lao Issara soldiers and soldiers from the regular Lao government. Up to this point, all the previous warnings told us to take cover at night, which we did. But now we were on the highest alert level. We had to evacuate the city. Grandpa Song would not leave because his son, Seng, and Seng's family did not have a vehicle to haul all their goods from the store, so he stayed behind. However, my mom loaded up the seven children along with her mom and Mom's five youngest siblings into her taxi, heading out south toward Pakse. Before we got to the only highway available, Issara soldiers stopped us, pointed guns at our driver, one of Mom's taxi employees, and told us to turn back to the city. Later, we realized the logic in these orders. Issara would feel safer if civilians were in the city. The French government military would be less likely to bomb the city with the population still living there, and we would be able to provide safe places to hide rebel soldiers. They were using us as a safeguard for themselves.

When we arrived back in Khongsedone, we drove by Uncle Seng's home, and there was a vehicle that Grandpa acquired from his daughter, Boualasy. Apparently, she had four vehicles but had not offered to share with the family. However, Grandpa Song apparently felt she could give one up. Growing up in China, my grandpa was known for his skill in martial arts. Though he was usually a man of few words, when he was determined, people usually complied. I suspect my aunt had no choice but to let one vehicle go for Seng and his family and their store goods.

We returned to our rented place next to my grandparents' home. Grandpa and Uncle Seng showed up with the borrowed vehicle loaded with their belongings. We stayed loaded in our cars until we determined where to go. Because the road south to Pakse was blocked, the only option was to try the other direction, which was north, toward Savannakhet. We watched some people drive north out of the city, and no one returned after an hour or two, so we thought this way might not be blocked. The problem with driving north, though, was that we had to drive right past our main house and right by the Laos government army camp, which was a potential target and quite dangerous to be near. We decided, however, that it was still the best opportunity for our escape, and we were willing to chance it.

Now we had two vehicles in our little family caravan. As we drove through the city, we saw French government army soldiers in their uniforms, with no Issara around; they had not yet penetrated the city, so it was still peaceful at this time. We drove past our home, and this was the last time we got to see Mom's dream home intact, for it was bombed later and was damaged extensively. After we passed our home, we approached the army camp, cautiously hoping to drive past without incident. The armed soldiers screened our vehicles and told us to keep going. What a relief! We were finally headed out of Khongsedone city limits.

The next village north was Napong, and Issara had already conquered this area. They stopped us there, telling us to stay put. We hid inside a villager's home for a couple of nights, but unfortunately, Tow was still a little baby and he was a little cranky, crying loudly no matter how we tried to comfort him. When he cried at the top of his lungs, an Issara soldier with his gun would peer into the window to see what was going on. This heightened my mom's stress because she was not able to calm Tow down. The Issara soldiers were preventing any cars from leaving the area, and we were becoming more and more afraid of getting caught in the crossfire of skirmishes. The Issara were known to use civilians to protect themselves. If they heard bombers flying near, they made the people get outside to be seen, hoping to avoid bombing. We were technically being held hostage for their protection.

At night we could hear gunfighting from Khongsedone, so we knew the fighting was drawing closer. A group of the detained civilians there in Napong decided to leave, gathering together, whispering to each other that someone had scouted a safe path to escape into the wooded area. No Issara watchmen were seen there. Grandpa Song took charge and told all his family that safety was the only concern now. At this time, we ditched everything except what we could carry. Even Mom's taxi and Uncle Seng's loaded vehicle would have to be left there. People whispered to one another, asking who wanted to join the foot caravan out of there. Before sunrise, a large group, hundreds of refugees, set out on foot on a gravel road, heading east out of Napong, continuing in Issara-occupied territory, toward the Xe Don River and my dad's hometown of Samia just on the other side. We crept out quietly in order to not attract the Issara soldiers' attention. Uncle Seng returned his borrowed car full of his belongings to Aunt Boualasy's family who were staying there in Napong. Uncle Seng later got all his belongings delivered to him by his sister's employees. Mom's driver stayed in Napong with our car and later joined us.

I was not sure where we were going in the dark with such a large group, but the leaders of the group knew how to get where we needed to be. During the dark and early morning, we traveled east, but eventually the leaders got off the road and took a rough trail through the woods. It seemed like we were walking, walking, walking through the woods, but the leaders were looping north and west, back to the main road. Finally, we came out on the main road where there was a taxi waiting to take us to Savannakhet. We loaded as many as we could get into the big, bus-like taxi. Several bridges had been burned by Issara, attempting to stop the traffic out of Khongsedone. When we would come to a ruined bridge, we would all have to get out and lighten the taxi so that it could attempt to creep across the rough terrain without the bridge. Even with these rough conditions, we somehow made it to Savannakhet that night.

In Savannakhet, my extended family stayed with my dad's old schoolmate from childhood, a distant relation and good friend, Pheng Chanthadoungsy. Even though my dad and Pheng had not been in contact for quite some time, Pheng took in Mom and all of us for a few days while we waited for news about my dad and his whereabouts. My grandparents and Uncle Seng's family found an abandoned building. The owner told them if they wanted to clean it up they could stay there, even though the locals believed it was haunted. Of course, no evil spirits bothered them, and they were glad for the shelter.

Pheng had many good connections because he was one of the highest-ranking military figures in the Savannakhet area. He tried to help Mom find information about Dad and his whereabouts. We heard all kinds of rumors and reports, all by word of mouth, which is not always the most accurate source. Eventually, we heard that the Issara forces had taken control of Khongsedone, and the French government troops, including the reserves, had retreated and scattered. We also heard that my dad had been shot. Another report was that some teachers had lost their lives in the battle.

Hearing these reports, my mom feared the worst and believed Dad was dead.

Pheng wanted to get to the bottom of all of these rumors, so he flew in an army cargo plane to Pakse to look for Dad and find out for himself what was really going on. Pheng learned that the rumors we heard were partially true, but to our joy, our worst fears did not actually happen. My dad was, in fact, injured, but he was alive—what a blessing for all of us. However, Dad's story was still very frightening, and he was lucky that his injury was not worse.

He and some other army reserves were stationed at a post with the fighting drawing closer and closer. They tried to radio for instructions, but the battery was dead. With no communication, they had no choice but to run for their safety. About ten or fifteen recruited teachers, including my dad, set out at night, headed toward another city outside of Khongsedone, hoping to avoid any confrontation or stray bullets. They traveled through wooded areas until they reached a stream named Hoikatin, which was close to my parents' farm. Dad was familiar with the area, and he was fairly certain the Issara soldiers were concentrated in Khongsedone, not out this far. He knew that they were nearing a town, but what he didn't know was that another French government army troop from Savannakhet was also in this area, headed to help in Khongsedone. Because Dad's group did not have any communication, they did not know who was nearby, and the French government troop could not know whether Dad and his companions were enemies or allies. The group's movement through the area alarmed someone, and a hand grenade was launched near them. Dad remembers being knocked down, and he immediately felt that he still had all his limbs. He was very thankful to be alive. He jumped up and began to run for his life, not realizing he was bleeding. The adrenaline must have kept him going until daylight came. In the light, he realized that the

Savannakhet troops were in the area, not Issara, so the grenade most likely was friendly fire from the French government side rather than enemy fire. His injury was not a life-threatening wound, but it needed medical attention. He somehow got to a Pakse hospital for treatment. I assume that the Red Cross traveled with the Savannakhet soldiers, and they could have transported him to the hospital. In their defense, they could not have known that Dad's troops were on their side when they were traveling in darkness. Issara soldiers did not wear uniforms, so even in broad daylight it would have been impossible to know where Dad's loyalties lay. Firing that grenade was a reasonable action for the situation. Pheng found him at the hospital and brought him back to Savannakhet in the cargo plane to join our family.

However, the same day my dad was injured, our family did lose someone. A teacher named Keng, who was married to my dad's niece, Thaim, in Hinsew, learned that the area was likely to be bombed, so he headed to the temple to warn the monk and others there to take cover. Often villagers would run to the temple courtyard to take cover during high alert, believing that sacred ground would be less likely to be attacked. Unfortunately, a bomb did drop in the temple courtyard, and Keng was killed. This saddened our family, of course, but it made us even more thankful to have my dad returned to us alive.

Pheng granted our family another favor. He arranged for us to return to Pakse. The only way to get there was to fly by airplane because Issara cut the country in half by taking Khongsedone. This was my first flight, and I was so excited to fly and be reunited with my dad. Mom had to bring her car through Thailand and across the Mekong River on a ferry to join us. We stayed in a small village along the Mekong River a few miles north of Pakse called Saphai with a friend of my dad's for a couple of weeks while Dad and Mom looked for a place to live. They found a home to rent there in Saphai. Our family took shelter there for about six months or so while we waited for our hometown to settle down. We had confidence that the French government would not give up on this area and allow the country to remain divided in half by Issara.

When the French government realized that the Khongsedone population had abandoned the city, they determined to regain the city and thus regain the valuable road to connect the country from north to south. Issara soldiers had fired at French government aircraft. If the French government aircrafts spotted any shooting activity, they would drop bombs in those areas. As a result, much of the city was in ruin. Our home had been especially valuable to the Issara soldiers who used it to hide out since it was so near to the government army camp, and it was targeted multiple times by the French government aircraft.

The Issara troops were forced out of Khongsedone and left behind a city in ruin. The war damage affected all aspects of living, including schools, hospitals, the marketplace, and all systems required for everyday living. Many unexploded bombs and land mines remained as hidden dangers to anyone who returned. Another unknown threat was that random Issara soldiers could still be in the city, so no one could possibly know whom to trust. Because of this, our family, along with most of the other residents, waited several months before returning to our home city.

chapter 7

Dodging Bullets

My fifth and sixth grade school years were not normal by any means. Instead of focusing on math, science, and French, we were focusing on each day's news reports, determining day-to-day how to stay safe from the intensifying war zone. We were figuratively and literally dodging bullets to stay safe. My fifth-grade school year had been so full of fear and conflict that I could not be promoted to the next grade, and this was the worst year this could have happened to me.

Sixth grade year was really the most crucial school year of all because this was the final year before taking entrance exams for further education. This was the year a student would need to review and refresh all subjects. My fifth-grade year had been disrupted from the war turmoil in Khongsedone and so many cancelled school days. I did not even finish the entire school year before Khongsedone was overtaken by the Issara. I spent my time dodging bullets rather than concentrating on school. When we were getting ready to start school in Saphai that fall, my dad suggested that we all be placed in our previous grade levels to be sure we did not miss any content. However, our teachers felt we were too advanced to repeat our previous levels, so they decided to move us up to the classes appropriate for our ages, disregarding my dad's suggestion. Then, of course, we struggled because we hadn't effectively covered all the material needed from the previous year. We were stuck between knowing too much and not knowing enough, but we stayed and struggled with students our same age levels as the school officials placed us.

Mom's lucrative taxi route had always run daily from Khongsedone to Pakse, but because Khongsedone was under attack, Mom decided this would be a good time to get the taxi repainted and have the motor rebuilt. The taxi went into the shop, and Mom found herself restless with no taxi route and no shop to tend. For once in her life, Mom was unemployed, and this was driving her crazy, so she thought up a new way to make money. Any time she would prepare food for our family's meal, she would make an extra dish. I would take the extra dish to the open market in town to sell. Mom would take the money from this sale and purchase more ingredients for the next meal. What a good way to stretch each dollar, or kip, as we called our money. The first half of my sixth-grade year was spent here in Saphai.

At first, my parents viewed Saphai as no more than a temporary place to wait out while our hometown was in ruin. Day by day we received accounts about various Khongsedone buildings that suffered damage, and even our own home was reported to have the roof blown off from bombs dropping nearby. The French government had battered our beloved city with bombs to clear out the Issara rebel soldiers, destroying so many structures. Before they would let citizens return to start rebuilding, the government wanted to clear out bombs, land mines, or other explosives that had not detonated. It was beginning to be clear to us that our return to our hometown would not occur any time soon.

Even though the schools and Dad's office in Khongsedone were closed with all the turmoil, he still had plenty of responsibility tending to several small grade schools still functioning in the nearby area. The education department created an office in Pakse for my dad to use for work. Consequently, our family's Saphai location was becoming a hardship for my parents. Mom started her taxi route again, driving from Pakse toward Khongsedone. With the school year starting, Dad would begin his workday in Pakse, and then he might end up in or near Khongsedone. My cousin Thaim came back to live with us after her husband was killed by the temple courtyard bomb. She cared for all of us in Saphai while our parents were working, but the travel distance was getting increasingly more difficult for my parents.

The taxi my dad sometimes used to commute between Pakse and Saphai had no regular schedule and was thus rather unpredictable. Most of the time when Dad got off work there was a taxi for him, but other times the last taxi had left hours before. On those occasions, my mom would arrive home, tired from her taxi route, and my dad would not be there. She would then have to drive the thirteen-mile route back to Pakse to look for him and give him a lift home. Mom and Dad had no way to communicate. This was long before text messaging, cell phones, or regular access to any type of phone, for that matter. Eventually, my mom and dad decided we needed to move closer to their work, so we moved to a suburb of Pakse called Thahin, where the taxi hub was located. Our rental home was walking distance from this hub. Dad often took a tuk tuk to work. Our location here was much more convenient for both parents.

Day-to-day driving was easier for my parents, but the move to Thahin meant that we had to begin in a new school in the middle of the year. Thahin schools were larger, and I had to get used to a system where I had a different teacher in a different room for each subject. I was used to staying in one room with one teacher for all subjects. Each class period had a different combination of students enrolled, rather than having the same students in class with me each period, supporting each other in our studies. I did not connect with the teachers or the other students; I felt isolated and overlooked. All this seemed a little overwhelming to me. I passed sixth grade, but I did not score high enough on my entrance exam to be admitted to high school or any professional field. The turmoil from the previous year had left its mark, and I was disappointed. I had never failed anything before, but I suppose I should not have been surprised. I was very detached from school and felt like I didn't belong anywhere.

By the summer after my sixth-grade year, people were beginning to return to Khongsedone. My family returned to Khongsedone in 1972 and stayed there until I was almost sixteen, when I had finished tenth grade in 1976. Thankfully, the government had driven out the Issara troops. Even though the city was torn and damaged from the bombs dropped to clear out the Issara, more and more people were returning to the area to rebuild and reclaim their lives. The area in and around Khongsedone was combed for land mines planted by Issara, and Route 13 connecting the capital of Vientiane to Pakse by way of Khongsedone was eventually opened again for travel. My dad had the responsibility of managing schools outside the Khongsedone city limits as part of his job, and he traveled to these schools more and more. Mom's taxi route was running from Pakse to Khongsedone, often giving Dad a ride one way or the other. At this point, my parents felt it was safe enough to return to our hometown of Khongsedone.

Much to our dismay, when we returned, we found our beautiful home was not inhabitable. Our yard had two or three huge bomb craters, the roof was blown off, and the walls were also damaged. Dad repaired it as well as he could, but we had to delay moving into this home for a bit. We moved into a rental house owned by my mom's matchmaking cousins, Khamma and Lop. This house was located within the city limits rather than the outskirts near the army camp like our home was. We were safer there, and for the first time, we had running water for four hours every day. This was such a luxury for us! We had no electricity, but we were so happy to have water available every day, even though we could not drink it until we boiled it. We rented this house for more than a year, and all this time, Dad was working to repair Mom's dream home. He longed to live in the open area, not in the crowded city, where, in his words, he had to "smell all the neighbors' garbage." He eventually repaired the home well enough for us to move back in, replacing the roof and most of the walls. The only original part of the house was the floor.

Because I could not enter professional school or high school, my parents paid for a private school to prepare me to retake the entrance exam. We studied math, science, and French there. The extra review paid off; I passed my entrance exam in the spring and began high school (seventh grade) the next fall. Khongsedone was safer than it had been during the war, but everyone was still a little uneasy or unsettled, not totally confident that unrest would not break out again. Instead of attending high school in Khongsedone, my parents sent me to live in Kengkok with my mom's sister, Aunt Boualasy, who was also my godmother. This was a good opportunity to attend a school in a larger city and better prepare me for future studies in medical school in Vientiane. I finished my seventh and eighth grade years there.

This was 1974, and it was a time of growing rebellion, turmoil, and uncertainty in Laos. Older students in high school and higher education began to hold rallies and protests, even though they did not even understand what they were protesting. At the time, these teenagers didn't seem to know what they were doing or have a plan they would like to see put in place. Little did they know that their protests that helped displace the French government allowed the new party to enter, and this party was the Issara, who were supported by the Communist government.

The new party was strong and was a direct threat to anyone who had worked for or supported the French government. The Issara government did not actually fire anyone employed by the former French government, but they did not have any budget to pay employees. Employees were expected to continue working but without pay. Government workers were previously considered middle class and were at one time more financially well off than farmers, but now they were beginning to suffer financially, with some not going to work, and some even leaving the country. For a while, farmers were in better shape than government workers because they were living off the land rather than entirely depending on a paycheck from the government. However, eventually the farmers suffered too when they could not sell any extra produce to purchase necessary supplies; there was no one with any money to buy from them.

Poverty was real. If you were fortunate enough to own something of value, you would live in fear of being robbed. People who might not have ever considered taking someone else's property sometimes became desperate enough to resort to theft. We could not feel safe owning anything of value. By this time, most of my dad's associates had not received a paycheck for two years, and they were extremely poor. People were getting thin, clothing was getting thin, and everyone's patience was wearing thin. Laos was becoming more and more unsettled, and if we did not see a friend's family for a more than a week, chances were good they moved to find work, or even more likely, they left the country. Government employees who had been required to fight in the military, like my dad, at first felt secure because they considered themselves professionals rather than soldiers. However, even these loyal citizens were targeted by the Issara forces. In

Issara's eyes, anyone who had carried a gun against their party was a threat, especially ones with management experience like Dad.

Even though my dad was not getting paid for his school administration position, our family was more fortunate than most due to my mom's trading skills. Her taxi was not profitable because most of her clients had lost their income and no one had money to pay to travel out of town. At this time, the Issara government began to realize how many people were leaving villages and cities, so they put restrictions on travel. People had to get permits to travel outside city limits, and check stations were put up at every city and village along the highway. Armed soldiers would ask for these papers, just like a passport at a border crossing. Travel was extremely difficult, if not impossible. Anyone who wanted to transport items such as food, salt, spices, or other supplies had to declare the items and the nature of the trip. If someone traveled with any item that was not declared, it would be confiscated. My mom and Uncle Seng in Pakse figured out a way to take advantage of the situation. Uncle Seng would spot some items in Pakse that he felt would sell in Khongsedone, and he would stockpile them at his house until we had proper papers to bring them home. Normally, the Issara government employees who monitored the permits to transport items would only allow enough supplies for one family's use. However, I befriended the wife of the Khongsedone official in charge of monitoring permits. Every once in a while, I would stop by with goodies from my mom's travels to share with the official's family. They were without a paycheck, so the treats were welcome gifts to the hungry family. As our friendship grew, I no longer had to visit the official's office to acquire exact permits to travel; I would mention that Mom was planning to go for supplies and I would get the paper, including the official signature and seal, but also with two or three blank lines so I could fill in with what we could purchase on Mom's trip. At first, Mom was making short runs, day trips from Khongsedone to Pakse to get supplies for us, and very little beyond this. We did not have vision beyond survival. As time went on, Mom learned more about how to increase her sales area and also increase her profits.

I had been living with my aunt in Kengkok, attending high school there for two years. Yes, I went to school to gain book knowledge, but the marketing skills I learned from my aunt and uncle during this time later became lifesaving skills for our family. At the end of my second year of high school, my parents brought me back to finish high school in Khongsedone. With all the unrest in the country, my parents felt it would be best for us to all be together in case we needed to escape. After I returned home, I was able to help Dad care for the younger kids, so Mom felt more confident that she could make overnight trips to buy and sell to the north of us, even as far as Savannakhet. She began to stockpile goods from the southern region around Pakse—goods that were not readily available in Savannakhet. She learned what she could take to Savannakhet to make a profit. We also started buying local products, usually food items such as eggs, coconuts, and whiskey—anything that would not spoil quickly. Mom would take these items to Savannakhet to sell, and then she would return with other items, such as clothing and seasonal items, to sell locally. At first, we were selling wholesale to store owners. This was enough income to keep our family fed and clothed, even though Dad had no income. Mom would occasionally make a little extra profit, and she would use it to purchase gold jewelry as an investment. Our economy was very unstable, and we heard rumors that the Issara government might get rid of the old French government currency (Lao kip). Silver and gold were the best ways to stockpile extra funds. Within a year, the Issara government got rid of the Lao kip and distributed equal amounts of new Issara kip to each family, so the Lao money was then worthless paper, only good for starting fires.

We were already under enough stress trying to survive, and then Dad got word that he would be transferred to Salavan, where the educational system was headquartered. It sounded like a nice promotion but was still without pay. Mom and the kids did not join him because we did not feel comfortable living in the midst of Issara's government. We also would have lost Mom's trading income, so supplying the day-to-day food needs for our large family would have been a great struggle there. We were under the impression that Dad was one of the Issara government important employees, selected to help run the education program there. Our home was located outside the Khongsedone city limits, and while Dad was there, Mom felt safe and secure. However, when Dad left, she grew a little nervous about the isolated location. The locals were growing hungrier and more desperate, and if they knew Mom had supplies, we were more likely to be targeted.

My maternal grandparents, who fled Khongsedone's war zone when we did, had settled for a time in Savannakhet. They eventually relocated from Savannakhet to Pakse and then finally back to Khongsedone. This helped encourage us to move into the Khongsedone city limits as well.

Mom found an open storefront within the Khongsedone city limits for our family to sell goods downstairs and live in the back and upstairs. She could sleep more easily at night without worrying about crimes against our family. Close neighbors made us feel more secure. This was a prime location for my mom, who liked to stockpile local goods to take to other cities for a profit. We were the first store for foot traffic coming up from the Xe Don River landing. We often spotted people walking up from the river carrying goods and offered to buy these goods from them. My brother and I often stockpiled goods for Mom while she was out traveling for her marketing business. When she came home, she would find a good supply of items for the next trip.

Some of my aunt and uncle's training I had learned in Kengkok was useful for our business. In Khongsedone, when customers would walk in from other cities, they would be tired, thirsty, and hungry. My aunt and uncle taught me to treat customers the way I would want to be treated. I would offer them the restroom, a drink, and food. I also befriended them, asking general questions and getting to know them, asking them their name and where they were from. It was very important to be able to call them by name next time they came by. I would offer them good deals from our store and some other stores I worked with. Living next door to a restaurant was beneficial. I could always supply a good meal for potential customers. It was well worth it to invest in these people. These new acquaintances would eventually bring their family members and friends, creating a network of customers. I had a different approach from many other store owners. Those owners would watch each customer closely to make them feel uncomfortable, assuming the person was trying to steal from the store. My aunt told me to notice if someone was stealing, but to not make it into a huge scene. If it's just an occasional item, that's a small loss, but the customer and all his or her friends and family will keep returning to buy your goods. If you ban that customer, your loss is far greater than the one stolen item.

Once I grew reasonably comfortable with someone in my network of associates, I would start to ask what sort of goods the customer might be able to supply for us to purchase. For example, this person might be able to bring extra eggs, dried hot peppers, fire torches, or honey from their home area. We might send these items to the big city to sell, and sometimes we might even sell the items in front of our own store, perhaps in smaller batches if they came in a large lot. One of the most unusual items to purchase from these traders was python skins. They would be stretched, dried, and rolled up so they were convenient to carry. We would pay by the surface area of each piece, and it had to be cut correctly with the pattern intact. Grandpa Song was our authority on the quality of the cut and the fairness of the price. If he said it was a good buy, we would buy it, and Mom would usually sell it to traders who would resell it in Thailand.

We stayed in this prime store location for a few months, and then two doors down, my grandma's sister Lan was leaving her store to move back to Pakse, so she offered for Mom to assume her lease for the store. Even though we would no longer be the first store up from the landing, we would have more room, and the storefront was more conveniently designed with shelves and display cases. It was a better arrangement for our business. My grandparents moved into our previous location two doors up, and this created a great setup for us when Mom was not home. I could take a sick sibling to Grandma's for a while to get special care. For a little while after our storefront move, when my customers would come into our old location, Grandma would try to act like that was still our store, and she would try to sell to them her own goods, giving the impression that the items were Mom's and mine to sell. I usually would notice my friends there, and I would bring them to our new store. I don't think Grandma fed them, so they probably suspected something had changed. Grandma was just trying to make a living, I suppose, and I think she was cute in her efforts.

I think of the friends I made in our Khongsedone business from time to time, and I wonder what they must have thought the first time they came back to our store and I was not there. I also wonder if they were able to continue selling their goods at a fair price after I was not there to trade with them.

With Dad gone all the time in Salavan, Mom slowed down

her trading activity, reluctant to leave us alone for any extended periods. Because we had a storefront location, Mom decided to test out whether she could profit from reselling Pakse goods at retail in her own storefront rather than selling wholesale to others. The trip to Pakse and back took only the day, so Mom would not be away overnight. After a few months of this setup, Mom began to buy more items, stockpiling goods to go north to Savannakhet. Her theory was if she could make a few trips there to get supplies at a lower cost for her storefront and also to collect items she could not find in Pakse, then our income would increase. Dad still did not get paid from his job, so we needed to send food items to him as well. Mom knew several people who were going to Salavan, and she could supply him with necessary goods.

The day trips to Pakse and back went smoothly but did not profit as well as we would have liked. We began to explore longer trips that might be more profitable. A trip to Savannakhet would require Mom to be gone for a couple of nights. A trip to the capital of Vientiane would take about a week. Mom finally tested her theory about traveling to Savannakhet to trade and found that she did, indeed, make a bigger profit in the selling there as well as the selling of Savannakhet items back in Khongsedone. She was able to continue the wholesale business as well as the retail at our own storefront. The blank permits we acquired from our friendly official enabled us to more freely purchase sellable goods. The only problem with this system was that when Mom was gone to trade, I had to be home to tend to the younger siblings and the storefront business. I missed schooling on those days. When my dad learned about this new schedule, he suggested that we find a nanny to work for us so I did not miss school.

When we lived in Khamthong, Mom and Dad had good friends who had a daughter, Noam, who was older than I was. They were without an income, struggling with the horrible economy like most Laotians were. Noam was happy to come live with us to provide extra money to help her family. We agreed on a price to pay her to help our family at that time. All and all, it was worth every penny. She helped keep us safe, I got to finish my high school education, and she was able to help her family in a time of desperate need. We were thankful for her service. Years later my parents were visiting my brother in California, and Noam came to see them. Noam told them she had opened her own store there, so we feel that she must have learned a few valuable tips about the buying and selling business during her time with us in Khongsedone.

After Noam joined our household, giving Mom more confidence that we kids would be cared for in her absence, Mom made her first trip to Vientiane. This trip was to scout out which of our local items were in high demand there. Items from Pakse and Khongsedone would often double in value in Savannakhet, but they easily tripled in value in the Vientiane market. Mom made acquaintances along the route there, and they became travel companions, often traveling on the same bus. With no hotels, these women would stay together at various homes, sometimes homes of friends, and sometimes mere acquaintances of friends. The women staying together offered more security. Mom's friends occasionally wanted to learn the buying and selling trade, and Mom was happy to train them. One particular lady friend started under Mom's training, and apparently, she learned well. After Mom left the area, this woman continued to buy and sell, gaining quite a lot of wealth. We heard she eventually owned some semitrucks to haul all her goods for her profitable business.

We all knew how unsettled the country was, and safe travel was not guaranteed. Mom certainly knew the risks. I asked once if I could accompany her to Vientiane because I had never seen the capital city. Mom said it was not a good idea for a young, pretty girl to travel this route. One day her intuition about the danger proved to be true. On the way back from one Vientiane trip, in the Lahanam area, the bus was stopped by men firing their guns in the air. Though they really did not know for sure who they were, the passengers assumed they may have been French government supporters who returned from Thailand to cause trouble with the Issara. These men directed the bus to pull into the woods, and all the passengers were demanded at gunpoint to leave the bus, walk into the woods, and lie facedown to not see what was going on. When the commotion stopped and Mom and the other passengers felt safe enough to get up, they went back to the bus and found their merchandise ransacked and stolen. Even though it was difficult to have so many items stolen, it could have been much, much worse. If any Issara soldiers had been on the bus, a shootout would have probably occurred, and the passengers would have likely been injured or killed.

In fact, a few years after this, one of my classmates was killed in a similar event when he was hit by a stray bullet. Mom's incident really scared Grandpa Song, who reminded my mom that she was the only parent around to raise her eight children and she needed to stop going so far for so long. She did stay home from Vientiane for a while but gradually returned to her travel plans. She still had to travel through the Lahanam area when she was going to Savannakhet, but Issara had added more security in that area to prevent this type of incident, making her feel comfortable enough to resume her travel. She made a few more trips to Vientiane, but not as often as before.

Our family tried to function as well as possible without Dad. We assumed he was working the same job he had before, just at a new location, so even though we missed him, we did not really fear for him. Dad was in Salavan for about six months before he returned to see us, and this visit began to plant some doubt in our minds. Two men with guns accompanied him and stayed at our house all the time Dad was there, about a week total. Was Dad losing his freedom, and we just did not know it? We thought he was working in an office, supervising schools, but these men seemed more like guards than coworkers. The next visit a few months later was exactly the same, with two armed companions staying with us again. His situation did not seem as harsh as others who had been taken to concentration camps. Those people did not get to see their families or receive news from anyone. Perhaps we were in some sort of denial, but Dad's situation seemed much better than this, so we did not panic at this time. Somehow, we did not realize that my dad was being closely guarded 24/7.

About this time, a few of my good friends had eloped with their boyfriends to Thailand, and though I really missed them, I understood why they took off. Then a fateful event put unbelievable pressure on me and my family. My classmates were rounded up and hauled away from their families to an unknown destination under the control of Issara, their families watching them leave with no way of knowing their destination and unsure of when (or if) they would see them again. These young people were all sixteen years old and, in the new government's eyes, mature enough to recruit for their own purposes. With my sixteenth birthday a few months away, I seemed to be the only one left behind. I needed to decide whether I would join Issara or escape, seeking freedom, and I could not wait long on my decision.

At night, Mom and I would whisper softly so the neighbors couldn't hear us. We discussed whether I should leave or stay. Mom even asked me if I had a boyfriend to elope with, but at that time, I did not have anyone I wanted to marry. Mom kept nudging me to go, and finally I agreed it was best, even though Dad's life could be in grave danger if the ones holding him knew what I was about to do. My safety, as well as Dad's, was at stake.

chapter 8

My Escape from Laos

Hushed voices whispered rumors about people we knew who were disappearing from the unsettled chaos in Laos. Thailand was the most likely destination for these people. We assumed they were safe in a refugee camp in Thailand. Third-world countries in Southeast Asia, including Laos, Cambodia, Vietnam, and Burma (present-day Myanmar), all suffered oppression in various forms, for the most part caused by Communist influences. Fortunately, the United Nations helped Thailand establish some refugee camps to hold those who were fleeing oppression from their own homelands.

Refugees from Vietnam had been fleeing to Thailand for years. At the time I left Laos, refugees from two of our neighboring countries, Burma and Cambodia, were also seeking safety there. Thailand was the only close neighbor country that the Communists had not been able to control. Thailand was much more advanced than Laos and the other small third-world countries in the area. Living in Laos during the 1970s felt more like we were living in the 1940s or 1950s, while Thailand seemed to truly fit into the 1970s. Their roads and buildings were stronger, the government did not harass citizens, and the economy was healthier. Hustle and bustle filled the cities and towns, whereas our Laos villages were very laid-back and quiet. Laos and other small neighboring countries were much easier targets for Communist interests than the stronger country of Thailand seemed to be.

My mom's sister, Aunt Tiane, was already in the Ubon camp in Thailand with some of her cousins, and I could go there to join her and be safe from the unrest in Laos. All of us knew that my mom's younger brother, Uncle Sisay, and his family had fled to Thailand before the refugee camp was established. With no refugee camp to offer a safe haven, he had to stay under the radar, basically hiding out. If authorities found him, he would be arrested. In fact, a few of his friends were discovered to be illegal immigrants and were put in jail. He worked for cash and did not draw attention to himself while he planned where he might be able to go for a permanent home. He and his family eventually moved to France, and this gave me the idea that Thailand could be a temporary home until I could find a place for a fresh start and a good future.

When I chose to leave Laos, I did not know whether the rest of my family would be able to get out due to my dad's circumstances. So as far as I knew, I was going out on my own at the age of fifteen. Even though my intention was to go to Thailand, Mom was planning to tell people that I was going to Savannakhet to live with Aunt Boualasy and attend trade school. This would be our cover story to keep Dad safe.

Once I agreed to go, Mom walked two doors down to whisper our intent to my grandparents. Mom's youngest sister, Luckmany, heard the plan and wanted to join me, and Mom agreed to pay her way too. Both of us got permission to travel to Savannakhet to live with Aunt Boualasy and attend trade school. This was believable and allowed us to obtain permission to travel to Savannakhet. Mom, Luckmany, and I arrived at my aunt's home in Savannakhet, where Veng, one of Aunt Boualasy's employees, asked what we were up to. Because we trusted Veng, we told him our plan and invited him to go with us. He said he did not have money for the trip, but Mom said she would pay his way. Luckmany and Veng would both help watch out for me. Mom felt more at ease this way because she knew I would be safer with two trusted companions going along. A young girl traveling by herself was vulnerable.

Luckmany is only about eighteen months older than I am, and we grew up as best friends. Veng and I had become friends when I lived with my aunt for my seventh and eighth grade school years. Though Veng was no relation to us, he later took our last name, Sonethongkham, so he could continue to travel with Aunt Boualasy as her nephew, even traveling to live with them in Canada years later. The three of us were very close.

Our escape route was to cross the Mekong River into Thailand, transported by two men Mom hired with some of her gold jewelry. At this time, Laos paper money was nearly worthless, but as always, gold jewelry never lost its value. Mom traveled with us right until the moment we stepped into that boat.

Escape from Laos came with many dangers. A high percentage of the families who came to Thailand had lost members due to the high risks of leaving Laos. Shady characters sought to take advantage of refugees as they attempted to escape, and many of these individuals were quite dangerous. It was common knowledge that those fleeing the country were carrying money and other valuables. The most dangerous assailants would even kill to get their hands on refugees' goods. We heard all kinds of horror stories of the journeys there. While many made it safely to the refugee camps, many others did not. Even some of those who were trusted and paid in good faith to carry refugees across the river were not always honest. We heard that some refugees were robbed by their guides, and others never showed up in Thailand.

Their families suspected that they had been robbed and then drowned to cover the crime. Girls were at significant risk to be raped, and if a girl was raped, she was often killed so she couldn't identify the rapist. Another grim threat to girls traveling at that time was being abducted to serve as sex slaves in the black market, which was all too common.

For the next few days, we stayed in the back room at my aunt's home in Savannakhet, more or less hiding out, while Mom lined up people she knew in the Lahanam area where we would cross into Thailand. My dad's family had settled in the Lahanam area when they immigrated from Thailand to Laos. Now, four generations later, I was about to travel the same route in reverse by leaving Laos to go to Thailand. I was headed to a refugee camp that was nearly in the same location as my great-grandfather's generation had once lived. I did not learn of this coincidence until Dad told me in 2018 while I was collecting information for this book. I really wish I had known about my ancestors' ties to the camp area when we were staying there. I might have wanted to explore the area and learn more of my roots.

We left Savannakhet by taxi very early in the morning one rainy day. We got off at a crossroad and walked toward a village. Once we reached the village, we were led to a house near the river where we would hide and wait for the opportunity to set out. There in the house, we joined a lady with two small children, as well as two young men and a girl. These people were also hiding and planning to cross the river with us. I was thrilled when I recognized the two young men. I had attended school with them for a couple of years in Aunt Boualasy's hometown of Kengkok. When I whispered in my mom's ear that I knew these two young men from my former school, I could see the relief on Mom's expression. Having more familiar faces, especially able-bodied males, to help protect us certainly was reassuring to both my mother and me. We really could not be certain that our paid guides were totally trustworthy, but the larger group kept us much safer. Now instead of only one man, there were three male bodyguards to help protect us. The odds were now in our favor if our guides had any intentions of harming us. We were also fortunate to have the young children along; most potential attackers would stop if they saw a small child.

It was the rainy season, and the Mekong River was rushing rapidly by us as we stood on the bank, but the inclement weather was actually a blessing for our plans. With all the heavy rain, the soldiers patrolling the Mekong River banks left their posts because they didn't want to get drenched. The people we paid to take us across knew the guards' patterns and knew this was a time they would probably abandon their posts. This gave us our window of opportunity to cross the river. Also, the pouring rain and thick fog helped provide cover. It was hard to see very far that day.

Was I scared? Yes and no. Now I look back, and I wonder how in the world I could ever have summoned enough nerve to step on that boat. But when you are a teenager about to do something, you don't really think about the danger. I knew I could be killed; all of us could have been killed, but in my young mind, I thought it probably would not happen to me. Also, I had Aunt Luckmany and Veng traveling along with me, so that boosted my courage.

At midafternoon, the rain was pouring down, and our paid guides said it was time to go. My mom had to say goodbye. Mom probably cried all the way back to the taxi and maybe even all the way back to Savannakhet, but my adrenaline kicked in, and I had no tears, only a rush to scramble down the river bank and into the canoe waiting for us. One guide sat in the front with a paddle to guide the boat. We made sure to put one of the strong young men right behind that guide to provide protection for all of us. Then we put the children in between adults, just in case the boat would capsize. Most of us were strong swimmers, but with no life jackets and a strong current, we just wanted to make sure the little ones were closely watched. Then we put my aunt's housekeeper and the other strong young male refugee directly in front of the rear guide who was paddling. Our logic was that if one of the guides planned to harm us, it would most likely happen from behind with the oar. Two of our guys sitting near this rear guide offered a reasonable sense of security.

As we set out, the guides told us, "Don't turn around. Lay low." This was creating the illusion that there were just a couple of fishermen out on the river to catch food rather than a load of escapees. The fog hanging thickly on the river and a driving rain also helped conceal us as we stayed low. If any guards on the shore would look our way, we hoped it would have been impossible to discern whether this canoe was loaded with a cargo of nine escapees or if it only held two innocent fishermen. In any case, we had to be silent and still to avoid detection.

The rainy season caused the Mekong to reach flood stage, so our guides were not paddling so much as simply guiding our boat between the logs and other debris, inching us toward the other side. It seemed the longest time since we were all bent over, breathing as shallowly as possible, only sneaking quick glimpses up before we heard, "Don't move," or, "Be still," hissed in our ears. The river was quite wide, and with mist and fog, we couldn't see much anyway. When we reached the Thailand border, we couldn't see our former homeland at all. In fact, when they told us to get out, we were not even sure if we were in Thailand or back on the Laos bank because we hadn't seen where we were going all this time. However, we had, indeed, safely crossed into our new land, the first step into freedom from the Lao Issara and their Communist influences that continually harassed and oppressed us.

One might think that entering Thailand meant we were free from harm. While it was true that we were safe from Lao Issara party persecution, we were now facing another precarious situation with the Thai government. Because we entered illegally without a passport or visa, we had no permission to be in Thailand. The Thai government could and would arrest us and place us in jail if they found us, usually for a minimum of thirty days. Before any refugee camps were established in Thailand, the procedure would have been to hold the illegal intruders in jail much longer than thirty days and then possibly deport them back to their homeland.

We all disembarked the canoe, each refugee with a small bag, and there we were. We were dumped out in a banana plantation, and we wandered around, lost, until dark. The plantation ran along the Mekong River bank, and it seemed like an enormous plantation. The giant-leaved banana trees were thick, and we could not tell which direction we were going. Perhaps the plantation was truly huge, but more likely we were traveling in circles. We circled around to the river more than once. Because we were all city-dwellers, none of us had much practice navigating through the wilderness. While we were wandering around, I realized I didn't have the bag Mom packed with some jerky and sticky rice. I had left it back at the house where we hid earlier that day. I was famished and so thirsty, but that was not the priority at that time. We fought the mud and mosquitos and were pretty miserable for several hours. However, when it got dark enough, we eventually saw a tiny light ahead. It was a rice farmer's kerosene lantern at his little hutch in the middle of his rice field. Rice farmers used these hutches as their shelter for a lunch break or as protection from bad weather. We could keep our eyes set on the small light in the distance, and that was our target. We walked to the light of the lantern and found an elderly rice farmer's hut.

We had heard of a refugee camp in Ubon Ratchathani, but we had no idea where that was or how far it was or how we could possibly get there. My older aunt, Tiane, was already in this camp, and our goal was to join her there. We would have to use our skills and resources if we were going to be successful. The first person we met, fortunately, turned out to be a valuable resource rather than a danger to our group.

This rice farmer was about to go home because it was dark, and he offered to take us to the house of a Laotian family who lived in his village. He thought they might be able to tell us what to do to get to a refugee camp. Getting lost and wandering around until dark seemed like a crisis at the time, but it was actually a blessing because when we finally reached this farmer, the guards patrolling the area were off duty. We walked right by their guard post without even knowing it as the farmer led us into the village, but fortunately, the watchmen were gone for the night. This prevented us from discovery by the authorities and almost certain imprisonment for a month or more for entering without legal documentation.

The area of Thailand we entered is known as Thai Isaan, part of the country that had belonged to Laos years before. The Isaan people there still felt a connection to our people, and when the opportunity would arise, they were willing to look the other way rather than turn us in to the authorities. They tended to protect and help Laos refugees. Once again, though, my mom's connection paid off when the rice farmer led us to the Laotian family's home. The lady of the house had a sister who traveled in the same circles as my mom. When I said who I was, she said, "I know your mom. My sister is a good friend of hers." There were no hotels in that area, and even if there were, we could not have stayed there without legal documentation. Asian custom was to lodge any travelers accompanying an acquaintance of yours. If you run into someone you know, or perhaps you are a friend of a friend, they are quite likely to take you in, so this worked very well for us at this point.

The house was a two-story dwelling. The bottom floor was open to allow more breeze to come through during the hot evening, and the family used this as their cooking and living area. After dark, when it was cooler, the family usually went upstairs to sleep in mosquito netting. They would lock this area, so this was where people slept for safety. We immediately went upstairs even though the evening was still quite warm. This way we stayed out of sight, and the family didn't look like they had visitors. The family members were accommodating hosts, scurrying around to prepare rice and other food items for us.

The next morning, we all ate breakfast with this family. The other six travelers were told how to avoid the police and get to the taxi station. Then they could figure out how to get to the camp on their own. Luckmany, Veng, and I were more fortunate because of my mom's connections. The protecting family knew that Cheng, my mom's relative, lived in a nearby town called Khemmarat. They escorted us in a taxi to get us to Cheng's house. The three of us looked enough like we were Thai that no one suspected we were fleeing Laos. We just had to remember not to talk, or at least try to sound as much like a Thai person as we possibly could if speaking was necessary.

In Khemmarat, we hid at Cheng's house for a few days while he left to telegram my aunt living in the refugee camp. Aunt Tiane and her future husband, Prasane, devised a clever plan to be sure we could safely enter the camp. She got three people to use our names when they requested papers to travel out from the camp. The officials there were not very detail-oriented, and they did not question the three imposters. No refugee had an authorized identification paper, especially one with a picture ID, so our word was all we had, and we definitely used this to our advantage. When we arrived at the Ubon camp, we walked right in without incident, but if anyone had asked for our papers, we were prepared. Documents with our names on them requesting permission to travel were on file there in the camp.

I had few belongings when I arrived at the camp. I didn't even have a backpack, just a bag with one outfit. This way people along the way wouldn't suspect I was leaving for good. I knew Mom had to use quite a bit of her gold to pay our way out of Laos, but she gave me some additional gold to use in case of an emergency.

In spite of the danger, the cost, and the journey through unknown territories, I had made it to the refugee camp safely. What a great joy! I was thrilled to be safe there, but then reality began to creep in and ruin my happiness. I was certain that the rest of my family would not be able to leave Laos due to my dad's situation, so I began to miss my parents and siblings terribly. Then more worries began to torment me. What if someone saw me here in camp and reported this back home? Regulations at the camp were rather loose. Sometimes people came from Laos to check on loved ones in the camp and then returned to Laos. My cover that I was attending trade school in Savannakhet could be blown, and Dad would be in danger. Also, I knew that my trade school cover story could only last for a year or two. After that, I should have finished my schooling and returned home. So even if no one reported seeing me in the camp, after two years, what would the government do to my dad when Mom's story of my disappearance was revealed to be a lie?

Uncertainty, doubts, and fears haunted me day and night for the first few months in the camp. However, these dark times would not last. My joy would eventually return.

chapter 9

More Family Members Journey to Thailand

Coming to live in the Ubon Refugee Camp area was, in a way, returning to my roots. My ancestors had a close connection here. My grandfather and his family had lived in this very area several years before my family and I came here for refuge. Apparently, we had a pattern of every third generation migrating in search of better lives, and at this point, my journey landed me right where my ancestors began, and eventually my parents and siblings would join me.

Our family's journey out of Laos was successful for a variety of reasons, including my mom's careful planning, her persistence to profit from her business, our family's connections to people who could help in various ways, our toughness and perseverance, and even a little bit of simple good luck.

Tay once told me that to him, our route out of Laos was similar to the Underground Railroad, and I think this is a good comparison. When refugee groups traveled through the area on either side of the Mekong River, to some extent, they were at the mercy of the locals. Some people in the area might have provided buildings to hide out, and others might have fed them. Most of the people in the area likely knew that these Lao travelers were immigrating illegally, but yet, they kindly turned their heads rather than drawing attention to these desperate refugees.

The first few months I spent in the refugee camp were the hardest time for me. I did not have much to do to occupy my thoughts, so I worried and fretted, making myself feel worse and worse. After about two or three months, we were very fortunate to have a special surprise. Aunt Boualasy, who was also my godmother, arrived in camp. Luckmany, Veng, and I were thrilled! She would serve as our guardian, so we did not feel so lost and alone. Aunt Boualasy also started preparing food to sell for profit, and she gave me work to do each day, which helped keep my mind occupied. This calmed me bit by bit.

I was in Thailand a few more months before the rest of my family began to arrive in separate groups. The second group to leave the borders of Laos included my dad and my two brothers, Tay and Tee. However, they were unable to join me in the camp immediately. They spent a little time as jailbirds before arriving at Ubon Refugee Camp.

The first ones to join me (even though they were actually the third group to leave) were the two oldest boys, Sing, who was fifteen, and Ott, who was thirteen at the time. Because Mom owned the storefront, she and any of the kids regularly had permission to travel to various towns to get supplies without suspicion. Sing and Ott obtained permission to travel to Pakse, where they went to the home of Mom's brother, Uncle Seng. The two boys then flew with Uncle Seng from Pakse to Savannakhet.

While they waited in Savannakhet for the time to escape, they hid out in old abandoned houses of family members who had apparently fled from Laos. Uncle Seng had the keys. During the day, the boys had to stay out of sight, but evening was a different story. Uncle Seng, who was probably about thirty years old at the time, enjoyed going out. They went to a movie one night, and they ate their meals out in restaurants rather than Uncle Seng bringing food to their hideout. In order to keep Sing and Ott from being noticed at the restaurant, he would ask if they could dine in the owner's private living area, near the back of the restaurant. That way, they were not around all the other patrons as they enjoyed their meal.

One time, though, they were definitely "caught" by someone who recognized them. Uncle Seng, like my mom, was in the taxi business. A family who lived near us in Khongsedone also had a taxi business, and they happened to be in the same restaurant as Uncle Seng and the boys. They were eating in the main dining area and would not have spotted them, except they had to use the restroom, which caused them to walk by the room where the boys were eating. The man tapped Uncle Seng on the shoulder and spoke to him. I am sure their hearts stopped for a brief moment to see the familiar face of an acquaintance from back home. He didn't actually accuse them of any wrongdoing, but he asked what Bouany's boys were doing there. Uncle Seng made small talk and said they were just there for supplies. The man asked if they might be heading to Vientiane 2, which was a sort of code for escape to Thailand. Uncle Seng stayed calm and brushed off the man's questions, but this chance encounter was disturbing. It had to unnerve Seng, who knew that the man knew what was going on. When the family got back to Khongsedone, whispers and rumors would spread about our family leaving. Mom would be pressured to get the rest of the family out of the country as soon as possible, knowing our secret plans could be revealed to the authorities at any time.

After about three days of trying to stay out of sight in Savannakhet, it was time for the boys to escape. The same people who transported Aunt Luckmany, Veng, and me across the river were hired to bring my two brothers across. Uncle Seng took the boys to meet up with the guides at the taxi hub, and this is where Seng and the boys parted.

The guides told Ott and Sing that they would be playing the part of the hired helpers on the taxi, stopping the driver to pick up customers, helping people in and out of the taxi, and

loading and unloading bags and various cargo pieces. This way, they would not draw suspicion about why two boys were traveling without parents. My brothers most certainly passed as taxi employees because they had helped Mom with her taxi services before. They were naturals for this role. Once they arrived in the Lahanam area, they left the taxi and stayed the night in the same house where my group stayed. They awoke hours before daylight and walked to another house. There they added two adult males and a woman. This woman seemed to have a connection with one of the guides, perhaps a mistress or girlfriend. Still cloaked in the predawn darkness, they all walked down to the bank of the Mekong River and slipped into the canoe. Everyone had a paddle. With the water rushing furiously, all of them paddled as hard as they could. Someone, possibly Sing, lost a paddle. The journey across the Mekong seemed to take such a long, long time. Time most certainly slowed down to a crawl with all the escapees fearful of being caught, but also the strong currents pushed them along in a diagonal rather than heading directly across, increasing their crossing time substantially. Finally, they reached the other side and took their first steps into Thailand.

Dawn was just beginning to break as the group began to walk through the same banana plantation where our group landed and wandered around for hours. However, the guides did not abandon them. They seemed to know where to go as they led the group to a taxi hub in a small town, and the guides accompanied the boys by taxi on to Khemarat. Mom apparently paid extra to have them escort Sing and Ott directly to the home of Mom's relative, Cheng, the same place Luckmany, Veng, and I had stayed.

They stayed there for a few days, working for Cheng in his business, helping make food products to sell, gathering water, and trying to appear as if they were there for a fun visit with relatives until they could find a way to get into the refugee camp. Cheng told them to try to blend in and not draw attention to themselves because they did not have legal documentation to be in Thailand. One day, one of my former classmates named Ehr showed up. Ehr was a resident of the Ubon Refugee Camp, but he was visiting his friends in Khemarat. While he was there, he heard that Sing and Ott were there with Cheng, so he decided to see for himself. Ehr escorted the boys back to camp. After a four- or five-hour taxi ride, they were dropped off at the camp entrance and walked "like normal" into the camp. Once again, the lax regulations worked in favor of my family, for no one asked for any sort of documentation as they entered.

When I left Laos, I believed I would live the rest of my life apart from my family. It was hard, but I was willing to do this to avoid the unknown future that Laos Issara would have forced upon me. Even though my godmother had joined me, the few months without my immediate family changed me. Up until that point, I often considered my younger siblings more of a burden than a blessing. However, the time away from them had made me realize how much they meant to me. I missed them terribly. Imagine my joy when I saw two of my brothers show up at the camp! This was my first glimmer of hope that my family, which had first been broken by the Laos Issara when they took my dad away, might one day all be reunited.

Dad's journey to freedom was even more frightening than mine or my brothers' because he had to escape from what was essentially house arrest by the Issara government. Just as I feared might happen, rumors were beginning to spread that I had been sighted in the refugee camp in Thailand, and this could be very dangerous, blowing our cover story that I was in Savannakhet with my aunt. If my dad was watched closely before these rumors, what would happen if those guarding him heard about his daughter leaving the country? His chances to escape would have been virtually eliminated. His travel would put him at an extremely high risk for prosecution and likely a death sentence if caught. When these rumors began to spread, I lost all hope of Dad escaping and allowing the rest of the family to join us in the camp. However, I underestimated my mom and her connections.

While Dad was living in Salavan under house arrest, he was not really imprisoned in a jail, but he was watched constantly, unable to leave his assigned house duties without a couple of armed guards traveling with him. This made it quite difficult for him to escape. My dad did not give them any reason to suspect that he might one day try to escape. He was patient and earned their trust for more than a year's time until an opportunity finally arose.

Dad's hometown of Samia was in the heart of Issara territory, and when friends and family members would travel to Salavan to trade, they would stop by to check on my dad, bring him goods, and bring him news of his mother's health. My grandma's health was failing, and her eyesight was gone. Because my dad could never be alone, those guarding him heard the news of Grandma's poor health, and this became an opportunity for my dad. He eventually received permission to go visit my sick grandma without the guards accompanying him. The government officials watching him trusted Dad enough to let him go see his mom back in Samia. There was no direct road from Salavan to Samia at that time, so Dad was going to have to take a roundabout route to get there. He would start at Salavan, take a taxi to Pakse, take another taxi to Khongsedone, and then catch a final taxi to Samia. The guards escorted him to the taxi in Salavan, headed for the first leg of the journey, Pakse. The guards watched him leave in the taxi, assuming he would eventually end up in Samia. He did complete the first leg of the journey as his guards believed he would, but even though he knew he was taking a huge risk, he stayed in Pakse rather than traveling on to Samia.

All during Dad's confinement, Mom and all of us would send supplies to help him out. The most important item in the box was Dad's cigarettes. Mom never wanted him to go without them. We were totally unaware of the health hazards then, so the supply box was delivered regularly. Laos had no real postal service at the time; in fact, houses did not even have a physical address. The only way to get the goods delivered was to hire a truck driver or to ask a friend who was going that way to deliver it for you. We had regularly sent the supplies this way with a friend. The guards were delighted to see my family's friend show up to drop off supplies because Dad would share all the goodies. They thought nothing of these regular deliveries. One final box of supplies arrived, and this time, our trusted family friend delivered something much more valuable than cigarettes and snacks; it was a whispered message that Mom wanted Dad to try to get to Pakse without any guards as soon as he could. This is how Dad knew that when the taxi stopped in Pakse with no guards watching his every move, this was his one and only chance to escape.

When Dad arrived in Pakse, he had a surprise waiting for him, compliments of Mom's younger brother. Uncle Seng was a Chinese citizen who was able to obtain permission to travel more easily than someone like my dad who had been employed by the previous French Laos government. Uncle Seng had a plane ticket purchased under his own name, and now Dad had to prepare himself for the biggest acting role in his life—one that meant life or death. He was about to assume my uncle's identity. He had to stay calm, look like he was legitimate, and not raise any suspicion that this ID was someone else's. Because the ID was for a Chinese citizen, Dad would act like he couldn't speak Lao well enough to communicate, and perhaps he would be believable.

The plan was to fly out on a plane from Pakse to Savannakhet. Ground travel was not an option. Law required taxis to stop at each checkpoint to be inspected in order to be authorized to continue their routes. Border patrol officials would stop every vehicle and could search any person at any given time for their proper documentation. Many people knew my dad in that region from his work with so many schools; he was very recognizable, so any number of people could identify him on the taxi and mention that he was there. When he reached our hometown of Khongsedone, the taxi route the guards expected Dad to take would veer off to Samia, not continue on to Savannakhet, so if someone saw him on the taxi route for Savannakhet, his cover would be totally blown. People would spread the word that he was not in Samia as he was supposed to be. The only way to travel out was to fly.

I suspect that the minute Mom got word that Dad made it to Pakse without the guards, she immediately enacted the next step of the plan. She took Tay, who was eleven at the time, and Tee, who was seven, to Pakse so they could leave Laos with Dad. Bringing the two boys along with him would allow him to travel with less suspicion. Once Mom had reunited Dad, Tay, and Tee, she returned home and let Uncle Seng take over.

Uncle Seng took the travel group to the Pakse airport, and when they arrived there, Dad grew increasingly more nervous. When it was time to board the plane, the loudspeaker called out my uncle's name, and Dad did not respond. Uncle Seng had to tell him that was his name called, so Dad had to act like he couldn't hear well to cover up for not responding to his announced name. So not only did he have to act like he could not communicate, now he must appear as if he couldn't hear well on top of that.

I later learned just how close my dad was to being caught and most likely beheaded from this attempt to evade the authorities. My uncle traveled frequently. The official at the airport was quite familiar with Uncle Seng, and this official recognized his name. He could have challenged my dad's identity. That would have been a certain death sentence for Dad. Fortunately for all of us, this official, even though he knew something was up, allowed Dad to proceed onto the plane under Uncle Seng's name. This was a crucial point in my dad's journey, even more critical than stepping onto the boat at the Mekong River. In this climate of corruption, the official probably did not receive much pay from his job, so he saw an opportunity to profit a bit from looking the other way as my dad left the airport. A while later, he told my uncle that he knew something was going on, and my uncle gave him a payment as a thank-you for letting Dad go through, basically paying a bribe to this official. In this case, our family benefitted from the corrupt society around us, and the bribe was a small price to pay for Dad's freedom.

Dad and the boys landed in the Savannakhet airport. After the close call in the Pakse airport, Dad was so fearful of being caught that he really did not function too well. For example, he was carrying a bag with a few clothes but, more importantly, enough money to get by for a few days while they waited to escape. Because of the low value of Laos currency, it took a huge pile of bills to be able to buy much. He also carried a few pieces of gold jewelry cleverly hidden in an empty toothpaste tube to use as payment in case of an emergency. Dad left the bag with Tay and Tee while he used the restroom. When he came out, they all began walking out of the airport, but no one remembered to pick up the bag. They walked out of the airport without it. Luckily, the family they were staying with in Savannakhet had a child who happened to be working at the airport. This young person had seen them there and somehow managed to pick up this bag and bring it home to my dad, who had not even realized they were missing it.

My mom had contacted the same people who brought me out successfully to see if they would be willing to take an even greater risk by delivering Dad into Thailand. Dad was so high profile that getting caught with him would have brought a certain death sentence to them as well as my dad. They agreed, but they would have to be even more discreet than they had been with my group.

Dad and the boys caught a taxi traveling toward the Lahanam area. Somehow, the plan to cross the river at the planned point did not work out; the guides did not feel safe to execute the original plan. The guides revised their plan, taking them to a different crossing point. They would have to go to the next village and catch a local taxi to go to the next town. Traveling in this local taxi would make them more likely to be detected as refugees. Tay remembers that they put on farmers' clothing to try to fit in, and it apparently worked, even though the city boys' skin was lighter than the farmers who worked long hours in the sun every day.

The people who were going to take Dad across the river had given him specific instructions to follow to get to the correct point, which was a farmhouse. The taxi dropped off Dad, Tay, and Tee, and they had to walk through rice paddies to the designated farmhouse. There they had to stay out of sight, waiting for the trailsmen to come get them when the area patrols would be less likely to catch them. Just like the day I left, it was raining hard. This helped my dad and the boys escape without being detected. Heavy rain is harder traveling most of the time, but this is optimal weather for escaping without detection. Rain washes away footprints, and if you can't see where you are going, then no one can see you either. The group was ready to go at a moment's notice, and the trailsmen arrived for them a couple of hours before daybreak. Typically, the guides waited until they had several people to take, and those people would share in the cost of the passage. Dad's timeline was so tight that he could not wait, so Mom must have paid the trailsmen as much as they would normally receive from several more refugees in order for Dad and the boys to get out right away.

Tay clearly recalls walking toward the river in single file. The trailsmen told them, "No talking! Do not step out of line!" They had a fear of mines in the area. This area had never seen war, so the fear was not from leftover war mines. Instead, Issara soldiers would sometimes set mines to catch people who tried to escape Laos. This is another indicator of how cruel this government was to their own people; soldiers sabotaged harmless families— citizens who were simply trying to flee the oppression. The group walked along the raised levee areas of rice paddies as they neared the river. Finally, the trailsmen stopped and dug out their canoe that they had hidden in leaves and brush.

They carried the canoe to the water, and the party set out across the river. Tay remembers that he and Tee had to bail out water from their canoe to keep the vessel afloat. The torrential rain was filling it nearly as fast as they could dip it out, using just their flip-flops as scoops. Debris such as limbs and logs swirled around them in the flooded river. Tay said it felt like it took forever to get across, but they finally reached Thailand, entering the banana plantation just as my group had done. They were cold and wet, and they could not even get a fire started to warm up and dry out, so it was a long night, indeed. When daylight arrived, the guides delivered them to a farmhouse, where they were all warmed and fed. I believe this indicates that the trailsmen must have had relatives or connections of some sort on both sides of the

Mekong River, enabling them to continue their services to those who wanted to leave Laos.

Once they were fed and warmed, Tay recalls the trailsmen and Dad having a heated discussion, apparently about money. The guide seemed to be asking for extra money, sort of like a tip. Dad had money stitched into a hidden place in his clothes, but he didn't want to reveal his hiding place. Mom would be likely to use the same guides when she left Laos, and she used the same hiding techniques. She did not want to be susceptible to robbery by these men. The guides knew that they would get the full amount agreed upon when they gave proof to Mom that Dad and the boys made it to Thailand. The proof for this trip was a puzzle piece, which would match with the other half Mom had in Laos. The guides would get this puzzle piece, take it back to Mom, and then they would get paid the amount agreed upon. However, these trailsmen seemed to want a little additional payment for themselves. Tay felt that because Dad did not tip them the extra money they wanted, the guides did not help them sneak past the police patrol stations down the road. Because of this, Dad and the boys walked right into the authorities.

Dad, like every other refugee who entered Thailand without permission, was subject to being arrested. We knew we were illegal, but all of us were willing to take the chance. Most refugees traveled directly to the camp without being noticed by Thai officials. Three of the four groups from our family avoided the officials. However, Dad, Tay, and Tee, unfortunately, were not so lucky. They had to serve their time in jail.

While the group was walking from the farmhouse, the police spotted them and arrested them for entering Thailand without documentation. The police loaded them into a cargo truck and hauled them first to Khemmarat, the northernmost district of Ubon Ratchathani Province. They were taken to a cell in a small jail there. Dad was required to stay in the cell, but Tay and Tee were allowed to walk out in the neighborhood to get food to bring back to the jail. They were kept there a day or two before they were transported to a nearby small jail in the Warin Chamrap area, where they stayed for perhaps a week or so.

The next transfer was to a much more intimidating facility in Ubon. Tay remembers being driven down a long driveway with men armed with Uzis standing guard along the sides. The huge gate opened to allow them to enter and then slammed behind their vehicle. Several long barrack-like buildings were lined up on the property. Outside the buildings, a rough-looking bunch of prisoners performed hard labor with balls and chains on their legs, all sorts of tattoos on their skin, and hard expressions on their faces. Officials assigned Dad and the boys to a building where they would sleep at night, and when they entered the building, it had open floors, not cells. When it came time to sleep, they all just spread out on the floor—no cots, pillows, or blankets. They were assigned to the second floor of their building, and at night, it was wall-to-wall bodies, everyone claiming their own area. Sleep was not easy. During the day, they hung out in the courtyard. Their food was cooked outside over an open flame, and they would line up to have some sort of stew, vegetables, or rice slopped onto a plate for each meal. Showers were out in the open as well, so they had no privacy there. Only males were housed there, no women or girls. In this high-security Ubon prison, each day repeated over and over. No one had told them how long they were to be imprisoned; it was just a waiting game to hear their names called to get out of there.

Finally, the day came when their names were called for them to be released from this facility. Their stay there only lasted about two weeks or so, but it seemed like an eternity to the three travelers. It was terrifying to be around such hardened criminals in a place where the death penalty was a common punishment. They were transferred to stay a few days in a much more comfortable jail with food, beds, water, and electricity. The rules here were much less harsh. A local man originally from Laos knew Dad and came to visit them in jail. Surprisingly enough, he was allowed to take them out for a meal. This acquaintance took a look at Dad and said, "What happened to you?" Dad was extremely thin and worn down from his monthlong journey out of Laos. He and the boys enjoyed the first good meal they had eaten in weeks.

I finally learned that Dad and my brothers were safe in Thailand when someone was released from the jail before Dad was. Dad asked this man to find our family members in the camp and tell us he was there. My aunt and uncle took me to see my dad and brothers in jail. Even though I had to see them confined in a jail, I was still thrilled that they were alive and well. I got to hug my dad for the first time in a long time. We just had to count down a few days until he could join us.

Although I had been taken by surprise to learn that Dad was safe in Thailand, my mom knew full well that he made it there safely. Transporting Dad across the border was extremely dangerous, and any trace of evidence would have been disastrous for those who helped him escape. Mom and Dad had figured out a way to ensure his safety without detection by authorities. Mom had to pay a larger amount for his travels, but she only paid part of the fee in advance. Then when the escape was complete, the hired men had to return to Mom with the secret sign (in this case, a puzzle piece) she had sent with Dad to signify all was well. Only then would they receive the rest of their payment.

After Dad left, Mom knew she was in danger, and she and the rest of the kids had to get out quickly before Issara realized Dad was not in Samia with his mother. She figured Dad's guards would give him approximately two weeks to travel and return from visiting his ill mother, and about a week had already passed. This gave Mom only about a week to execute the rest of the plan. At this point, she delivered Sing and Ott to the guides for their travels. She then was left with herself and the three youngest to escape.

Once Sing and Ott left Pakse with Uncle Seng, Mom went home to Khongsedone to get the rest of the kids and to grab a few things. One important task she managed to complete was returning the deed for our family farm to the previous owner so that the government would not take it over. She also enlisted our nanny to keep our storefront open for a while to cover for Mom's departure. The nanny had run the store before without Mom there, so that would look normal. Mom let her have anything she wanted from the store as payment for her help. When Mom was safe in Thailand, someone gave our nanny the okay to leave whenever she wanted. The Lao Issara government took whatever was left after that. All of Mom's business assets she worked so hard to build became of no value to her, even her taxi. The value of our possessions paled in comparison to the value of our lives and our freedom. The only thing that mattered now was for her to avoid raising suspicion in the community. Without the full household of noisy young children, people might start asking questions about where everyone was. Even the most innocent comments from those who did not intend any harm to us could fall on the wrong ear and raise suspicion from officials, and she could not risk that. She would not linger, but instead, she would get the rest of them out as quickly as possible.

Mom was under extreme pressure to leave immediately, but she had forgotten one very important item that delayed her escape for a couple of days: Noi's blanket. Noi, who was just a year old, was inconsolable without his blankie. My sister Nang (eight) had already been delivered to my uncle's house in Pakse to spend a few days. According to Nang's writing, my talkative sister had nearly exposed all of Mom's plans for our family's escape. Mom had to quickly remove her from Khongsedone to be sure that she would not have an opportunity to give away any more family secrets. My mom, Tow (five), and Noi left Khongsedone for the final time to join Nang in Pakse. After one night there with Noi crying nonstop, Uncle Seng worried about Mom's safety traveling out of Laos. Noi could possibly give them away when they were supposed to be quiet. My uncle suggested to leave the baby with him so the rest of them would have a better chance to escape. Of course, Mom was completely against this idea. Instead of remaining hidden, she risked being caught by going to the taxi station to get help, right in full view of everyone. She enlisted help from one of her friends who had a taxi headed to Khongsedone. She asked her friend to stop by our house to get Noi's blankie from the nanny who was still there running the store. They already had the plane ticket purchased and were on the way to the Pakse airport, but they still had to wait at the taxi station to meet up with the friend to pick up the crucial blankie. This was a huge risk on my mom's part. This friend could have easily let it slip to someone else that something was going on with Mom, and that bit of news could have reached the wrong person and alerted authorities about her plans. This is the kind of mother we had; she put her own life at risk to keep all her children under her wing, even a crying one-year-old baby boy. Traveling was difficult enough without this delay. Mom was almost as recognizable as Dad from all her trips back and forth for her marketing trade. Having the three kids and no supplies would have certainly triggered many questions at the checkpoints because those who worked there were so used to her driving through with lots of goods and no children. Just as it was with Dad's group, flying was the best way to keep Mom's group from being noticed, and it also made the travel time shorter.

Mom planned to leave from Savannakhet just as the previous three groups had done. These guides had been successful so far, and Mom wanted to keep our family's escape as quiet as possible, so new guides were not a good option. Mom had to leave the kids there with Dad's distant relative in Savannakhet so she could find these men and make plans for them to take them across the river. Mom had to instruct Nang to be very cautious and not talk to anyone while Mom was away.

Until this time, Mom had been fairly calm and was able to execute her plan for all of us with strategy and clear thinking. However, her window to complete the plan was about to close because Dad's permission to visit his ailing mother was about to run out. His Issara guards were probably just about to come looking for him, and if they found he was not there in Samia, Mom's life would be in danger. Mom needed to wrap up her plans quickly, but she was at the mercy of the hired men's schedules.

I do not know many of the details of how Mom and the three little ones made it into Thailand. Mom had never seen a Bible, yet her Grandma Vadd had taught her to pray to a higher power. Mom's prayers were general, never uttering the name of Jesus, for she had never heard of Him or realized that He is the Son of God. So even though she did not know to whom she was praying, she must have felt comforted and close to her grandma as she knelt by her bed each night to pray for her children's protection.

One of the details Mom shared was that they were also stranded on the banana plantation just as we had been. Mom confessed that her only regret in our journey was that she had not kept one or two older children back to help with the youngest ones as our family's final group escaped. Nang was barely big enough to help as they struggled to carry Noi and urge Tow to keep up. Fortunately, even at this young age, Noi seemed to understand he needed to be quiet. He did not make any noise to give them away, and on the boat, he stayed still, causing no commotion. Of course, having his blankie helped, but I think he was probably scared and sensed the danger around him.

Mom, Nang, Tow, and Noi finally joined us in the camp at Ubon to make our complete family of ten. We were blessed beyond belief to be together again. So much was at stake for our family as we fled to Thailand, and all of us are extremely thankful to be here in America now.

As I gathered memories about my family's journey from Laos, it became clear just how many people risked so much to help us. One person, though, stands out. Uncle Seng was the one who helped plan our escape, delivered us to our destinations, protected us, and even risked his own life by putting his name on Dad's plane ticket and paying hush money to the airport employee who knew something was going on. He did all this so that our family could find a better life together, free from oppression. As youths when we escaped, Ott, Tay, and I were aware that Uncle Seng assisted us, but until we collaborated for this writing, we had somewhat taken this assistance for granted. As we shared our individual stories with each other, we began to realize the extent of his help as well as the risk and the danger he faced for his part in our escape. We are forever grateful to Uncle Seng for his unselfish love and support.

chapter 10

Nang's Story

$\mathscr{I}$n honor of my beautiful sister's memory, I feel compelled to share her last writing, submitted just a month before she unexpectedly died in 2006 at age thirty-eight. She had written these memories for her college English class as she continued her education. Here are Nang's own words about her journey from Laos:

Leaving Laos
Nang Soudavanh

Sometimes it took a life challenge to appreciate the character of a person. My mother was faced with one life challenge: to get our family out of the turmoil in our country. Because of her love for our family and her belief in keeping our family together, my mother was determined to remove our family from Laos. At a young age, I traveled with my mother and my two young brothers out of Laos. I learned to understand the reason for my mother's determination: to keep our family from being mistreated and from us mistreating others.

It all started in 1977; two visitors came into my third-grade classroom and said, "To protect our country, we need your help. We want you to observe your friends and family and report any special activity." Not knowing what the visitors were asking, I raised my hand. "My older brothers and sister have been vacationing with my mother." The comment seemed harmless. When I got home, I intercepted my mother from her vacation. Mom came home without my older siblings! With excitement, I told her about school, the visitors, and what I told the visitors. Mom was upset. At eight years old, I did what I was told, "To observe and to report." I did not know that mom was in the middle of executing her plans to save our family, her plan to take the last group of her children out of the unstable Laos. Mom took us through a journey in preparation to leave the country. During this journey, I saw Laos's encountering problems: posing a curfew on its people, facing an inflating economy, and, most important of all, mistreating its citizens.

During this period, Laos posed a curfew on its citizens, no traveling without permission and no traveling after dark. The next day, I showed my next-door friend my permission slip to travel to Pakse. We were on the road as soon as the transit came into town. The transit came to a checkpoint, and the armed guards ordered everyone out of the vehicle. They checked our papers and demanded to know the nature of our travel. Mom replied, "My daughter and I are going to Pakse for a haircut."

After a half day of traveling, we got to Pakse. Mom spent most of the day talking to Uncle Seng, and I was not allowed to interrupt. The next day, Mom returned to Khongsedone (Kong-se-done). While waiting for Mom, I spent many days helping Uncle Seng at the bazaar selling silk fabric and clothes. Because the economy was so inflated, most customers bought two yards of fabric with a diaper bag full of cash. Instead of keeping my eyes on the customers, I was watching Uncle Seng counting and changing the customers. Uncle Seng preferred silver or gold as a form of payment over suitcases of paper money. The process of changing the customers was time-consuming!

After a week had passed, Mom arrived with my two younger siblings, Noi and Tow. Apparently, Mom forgot Noi's baby blanket, and Noi spent most of the time crying. Mom told Noi, "Someone will deliver it tomorrow." The next morning, Mom told me that we were going to visit Aunt Phomphet (Pom-pet) in Savannakhet (Sa-van-na-ket). She instructed me, "Let me do all the talking." We intercepted Noi's blanket on the way to the airport. For the first time in our lives, we flew in an airplane!

Although it was so nice to see the blue sky and the fluffy clouds from the airplane window, I couldn't help but miss my father. This was the first trip I took without him. The last time I saw my father was a year before; he was allowed to come home one week per year. In 1974, the government of Laos switched to Communism; my father had been mistreated. Dad had been deprived of his freedom. Along with the people who performed civil duties for the replaced government, many peaceful men and women were sent to be brainwashed and taught to be submissive citizens. My father, an educated man, was sent to be reeducated in a reeducation camp. My father's duties with the old government were nonmilitary; he took care of the education program in the southern province of Laos. Dad was considered one of the lucky ones since the duties he performed were related to a household servant. As a servant, Dad gathered firewood, tended to gardens, fished, cooked, and cleaned.

The airplane landed in Savannakhet, and we took a taxi to Aunt Phomphet's home. The house was empty! The neighbor recognized Mom and walked over. He told us, "Phomphet and the whole family have been gone for two weeks now. Rumor has it that they left Laos for Thailand (Taii-land)."

In my heart, I prayed for the safety of my aunt and her family. The neighbor continued, "We heard they made it safely to Thailand." Mom let out a sigh of relief, and I did too!

Hearing that brought back an incident that occurred in Khongsedone a month earlier. A man was whipped and paraded through the town. Amahit (A-ma-hit) did not live in Khongsedone, but he was being prosecuted in our town. The look of Amahit was a sight of the crucified Christ. Both of Amahit's hands were raised upward and tied to a post above his head. His head cocked to one side and showed signs of unconsciousness ... His body was dangling since his feet could not bear the weight. His knees slugged forward, and his toes twisted inward. Through the center of town, a water-buffalo-drawn wagon carrying Amahit was driven by military personnel. Two young soldiers, who were not much older than my siblings, took turns whipping the captive. Through the intercom, a military official announced his crime. He stated, "If a crime is committed, any citizen is subject to the same treatment!" The officer went on, "This man got caught leaving the country!"

For many days, the town folks thought the only crime Amahit committed was trying to leave the country. Later, we heard that Amahit was caught stealing a chicken from a farmer. We also heard that Amahit was involved in a murder. A murderer or not, Amahit was prosecuted without a fair trial!

This was the second display I saw in the last month. The whipping was hard on my mother. For days afterward, I heard Mom up nights; this was not uncommon ever since my father was taken to the reeducation camp. It was an additional blow since she imagined her boys in the place of the young soldiers; Mom gave my older brothers daily lectures on the fair treatment of others. It seemed a few days from that incident my mother started to take my siblings on vacation; she started from the oldest to the youngest.

We spent three days in my Aunt Phet's abandoned home. Each day, Mom became more nervous. Sensing her being uneasy, I knew that Mom wouldn't be taking us back to Khongsedone. More than missing my hometown and friends, I missed my five other siblings. Since I had not seen them in Savannakhet, I suspected they might have left the country. It seemed everyone we knew was leaving Laos. With enough courage, I asked Mom.

She said, "They are safe and away from danger." A smile on her face confirmed my suspicion.

Although our stay in Savannakhet was short, we performed two routines. Our daytime routine started with my mother leaving us at the abandoned home. The kind neighbor fed and took care of us. In the afternoon, we walked with the family to the sugar cane field. Their father chopped and peeled the sugar cane stick and handed each to us. The sweetness from the juice was refreshing!

Our nighttime routine started with Mom returning to the nest to comfort us. After dinner, Mom taught me to sew. It seemed an odd time for a sewing lesson. Because of Mom's short temper, I complied and learned quickly.

The process started with Mom removing the hems of each of our pants, shirts, and underclothes. Then she inserted each piece of the 24K (karat) jewelries of Thai money into each opening. Finally, she handed the clothing to me to sew the hems together. After the last jewelries were hidden, Mom softly commented, "This is all we have to live off."

On our last day in the abandoned home, Uncle Seng from Pakse showed up with Mom and took us to another location. We arrived at the home late, so I don't know what the outside looked like. Mom ordered us, "Stay away from the windows! We don't want people to see us. In two days, we will be traveling."

Uncle Seng showed up with each meal. One morning prior to the sun rising, Uncle Seng led us into a rental vehicle and bid us farewell. Around noon, we were dropped off near a hut in the middle of the rice field. We were greeted by a middle-aged couple who said, "*Sa-bye-Dee* (Hello)." After they fed us lunch, a gentleman led us onto the rice paddies. Before we knew it, we were at the edge of the Mekong River. A small fishing boat was waiting to load us. While Mom was helping me into the boat, I heard her say, "This is it!" Like the folks we knew, we were about to do the same thing—cross over to Thailand.

A few days later, my suspicion of my siblings came true. As we were walking into the refugee camp in Ubon, Thailand, they greeted us. Along with the five siblings were many relatives as well as one man I longed to see: my father! Thinking back to Mom's words, she should have said, "This is the beginning!" My mother's determination as well as her love for her family gave her the strength to act quickly and to end the harsh environment in our life.

Mom, thank you for your gift of freedom, a wonderful gift to my father, my siblings, and me.

chapter 11

Life in Ubon Refugee Camp

One might assume that a refugee camp would be a grim place and that the time spent there could be filled with uncertainty, danger, and hopelessness. This was definitely not our experience. The time we spent at Ubon Refugee Camp was so much easier than our lives in Laos; all ten of us were together at last, free from the oppressive Issara rule and Communist influence in our homeland. In this camp, we would fall into a routine and begin working to find our future homeland, searching for opportunity to create better lives for us all. My brother Ott has shared with me that the time we stayed at Ubon Camp was really one of the happiest, most carefree times of his life, and most of us would probably agree.

At the camp, we first stayed with Aunt Boualasy until Dad could build a bamboo hutch for shelter. Our hutch was built with a straw roof and bamboo outer walls. My dad built it a little bigger than most of the other hutches in the camp because there were ten of us, and he also planned to hold classes there. The kitchen and the classroom had dirt floors, but our bedrooms and our dining area had bench-height bamboo flooring so that we would not have to sleep on the ground. This protected us from snakes and other threats. The small bathroom and shower area had concrete flooring. We did not have electricity or running water there, so my brothers' main job was to supply water for our family's use. The boys would take two buckets each, either attached to a pole and carried across their shoulders or else carried one in each hand, and go to the well assigned to our group in the camp. They would carry it back to our hutch to pour in the concrete reservoir dad had built. Some days they had more trips than others, depending on whether we were washing clothes or if the boys decided to shower at home rather than dumping water on each other at the well site.

After about a year or so, we outgrew our hutch and had to build on. Mom's parents and two youngest brothers missed having Mom living nearby in Laos, and they requested to move to Thailand. Because they were Chinese citizens, they could travel as they wished as long as they would give all their assets to the Lao Issara government. They followed us to the refugee camp and moved in with us, prompting Dad to build on a room for them. Instead of ten mouths to feed, we now had fourteen.

My mom had brought some gold, which she used to get some food for us. We were so glad to be together that nothing else much mattered. Then reality hit. We had to eat for more than just a day or two. Each family was registered in a group according to the number in their family. We received a subsidy of rice for the family once a month, and we were so thankful for this donation. As Asians, we ate rice with each meal, so this helped us immensely. An organization (I am not sure who it was) attempted to provide additional food items, but they did not have a refrigerated truck. Most of the food they brought was spoiled, and we really couldn't eat much of it.

Mom and I tried to think of a way we could get money. We decided we could take a taxi to the city of Ubon to purchase food from the market there. We made enough that we could feed our family and have some extra to sell. Some of the refugees had found low-paying, labor-intensive jobs in the area surrounding the camp. They normally had rice to take with them for lunch, and they would purchase some small portion of food from us to go with it. With extremely low wages, they could not afford to spend much, but they bought a little from us. It wasn't the perfect answer, but it stretched out our resources a little bit. Some of the refugees had family who had already been able to leave the camp, had settled into a new country, and could send a little money to help. Some of the refugees came with money, perhaps a little, or perhaps quite a bit. People knew how to survive. Thai language was very similar to Lao, but with a few twists that could throw me off in my trading at the market. I had a Thai and Laotian dictionary to help me figure it out. I learned a little bit of Thai this way, and this came in handy.

As the sun set in the evenings, people at the camp would get out and walk around, socializing with one another. Some people began to prepare various food items, and they would sell them for a small profit to others during this time, almost like concessions at a fair. The area used during the evenings for these stands would be empty each morning. I talked Mom into fixing some dishes that workers might purchase to take with them for their lunches as they were leaving the camp early in the morning to go to their day jobs. I selected a stand located near the camp's main gate where people went to catch a taxi. This became the beginning of our buying and selling adventures in the camp. We eventually expanded our offerings. When we went to market to buy groceries to make dishes to sell, we bought extra items and put some of the fresh groceries out to sell. After a couple of days, we realized there was a market for these goods. People were eager to buy groceries from us, even at a higher cost, because they saved on taxi fees and time. So we might purchase two chickens, with the intention of selling what we could to someone in the camp, and then our family eating the rest at a reduced cost to us.

When people in the camp saw our success in our sales, other families began to join in on the selling in this area each morning, earning income for themselves. The morning market was so popular that the area became congested and a little chaotic, getting more crowded each day. Camp officials decided to designate a specific, vacant area at the back of the camp for morning market stands. After this area was zoned for market, no one could live there. Up until this point, I did not have a stand of my own. I perched at any stand that was closed at the time. With this newly zoned area, my mom and I had a little stand of our own built by my dad. By this time, with our own stand, we could purchase larger quantities. Instead of just two chickens, we might purchase two dozen chickens. On other days, we might bring a quarter of beef or half a hog from the Ubon market to cut up and sell by portions there in camp. I became very skilled at cutting up meat into just the right portion for the customer. We also provided lots of fresh vegetables. In Asia, our meals were planned with the vegetables first, and then we added some meat to go with the vegetables, which is usually opposite of our meals here in America. We would even sell soup bones for the local soup stand. Mom and I can take credit for being the ones to start the Ubon Camp Farmers' Market during the time we resided there.

Even though Mom and I were pretty good at stretching out our money, we still had to occasionally use some of Mom's gold jewelry to supplement our grocery fund. My grandparents helped some with the groceries, but sometimes we did not sell all our goods, and we ended up eating more than we should rather than profiting from our products. Eventually, we were running out of money to purchase supplies in town for resale in the camp. Mom was worried to the extent that she finally wrote a letter to her brother and sister who were living in France, asking if they could loan her some money. She promised to pay them back when we got to the United States. Both of them sacrificed and came through with money to help. Aunt Tiane, who lived near Paris with her husband, Uncle Prasane, sent us money. Uncle Sisay and his wife, Aunt Bouakeo, lived close to the Germany border, and they sent money as well. Uncle Sisay worked overtime every chance he got to make extra money to send us. Aunt Bouakeo told me that Uncle Sisay would not buy himself new work shoes that he badly needed; he just inserted some cardboard to make his old pair last longer so he could send us more money. Uncle Seng had helped us tremendously in our escape from Laos, and now these aunts and uncles helped to keep us from hunger while we were in the camp. Mom kept track of how much they sent and repaid them in gold once we were in the United States. Mom would figure the value of gold according to the money we received, and then each time they would come to America to visit, Mom would send gold jewelry home with them until the loan was paid off. We are very thankful for their generosity.

Most of the people in the camp spoke only Lao. Most people began to realize that they would need to learn a second language when they were ready to leave Asia. Laos had been colonized by France for several generations, and you might assume all Laotians could speak at least a bit of French. However, students learned to read French but never learned to communicate with the language. Dad knew enough to help with the basics of learning the language, such the alphabet, counting, basic word meanings, and sentence structure. He started a little class at our house to teach people French for a small fee. Some couldn't pay, so Dad didn't make much money, but every little bit helped our family.

Ubon Camp was originally a military base, with a main paved road and then areas divided into sections by mounded ridges. Each area was designated as a numbered group. Then each dwelling was given a number. We lived in 18 in Group 13. The military base had several permanent structures, which were long, warehouse-like buildings. Hundreds of people could live in each one with little privacy, each family divided from another family by mosquito nets or hanging blankets or fabric. However, by the time my family arrived, those buildings were overflowing, so we did not have a chance to squeeze in there. Dad found an empty spot and erected our shelter there in Group 13. The back of our hutch was against the mound that separated our group from the next one.

We felt safe here. A good fence surrounded the camp, and the Thai government supplied officers to patrol the front gate, closing it at night and opening it in the morning. If we wanted to go out after hours, we had to have permission; we couldn't just come and go as we pleased after hours. This offered us security from intruders. Only rarely did criminals bother our people when we were here. *Cammoi* means robber or intruder, and when we heard someone called that word, we knew that person was in serious trouble. One young Thai troublemaker came in to steal from some of the refugees, but he did not make it out alive. They tossed him out the gate, and I am not sure who picked him up. I learned that you do not ever want to rob someone who has very little to lose.

All during my flight from my homeland until this point here in the refugee camp, I had stayed strong and fearless. However, my breaking point finally came, not because of fear for myself, but for my dad. In fact, the only time I ever cried during the whole ordeal of our family's escape was when I was safe in the refugee camp, before any other family members had joined me. One day a close family friend whispered to me that there was talk in Khongsedone about me. She said that someone had told her that I was spotted in the Ubon camp, and rumors were spreading that my mom's story of me being in Savannakhet was not true. This could be very, very damaging to my dad's safety. If his Issara captors learned of my escape, they could punish him for my crime, and they could be brutal. I fell to my knees, sobbing inconsolably to think I could have caused my dad any sort of harm. Until this point, I had held hope that Mom could bring the rest of the family into Thailand to join me, but now I was certain that I would never see my dad again, and this was more than I could handle. I was devastated, just like my grandma had been when we moved away from her home in Samia. This state of despair was a dark heaviness that I could not shake, and it began to take a toll on me. The anxiety weakened my body, and I became very sick.

We did not have any medical care while we were in the camp in Thailand. Over-the-counter medicine was all we had there. I had a high fever and could hardly move, symptoms that resembled malaria, but no one diagnosed it. I must have looked like I was at death's door, because even though we really did not have the money, Aunt Tiane and Uncle Prasane were concerned enough to seek medical attention. Uncle Prasane formerly lived with a friend in a house outside the camp, and he had connections in the area. He knew of a clinic in Ubon, and he took me there. I was probably dehydrated because I felt better after I had an IV in the clinic. I am pretty sure we never paid the bill there, so the medical staff must have treated me as a favor to my uncle. I am thankful for their willingness to put my life ahead of their pocketbook. I wish I could have paid for the lifesaving treatment I received, but all in all, I am very thankful for Uncle Prasane's connections and the provided care.

Overall, life in the refugee camp was happy once we were reunited. I kept busy finding ways to profit with the market business, but my younger siblings had only a few responsibilities without schooling to take up their days. They could play and relax more in the camp than they ever could in Laos. Ott has mentioned that the time spent in the refugee camp was perhaps the most carefree time in his life. He also reminded me that sometimes buses of school children would take field trips to drive through our camp to see firsthand what a real refugee camp was like. These Thai students had a chance to witness history taking place in the form of their homeland's action to offer safe haven for refugees, even though it made us feel a little bit like zoo animals on display.

Though we were content there, we still knew we needed to find a new country to call home. My dad had worked for the French government, so we could have had an express permit to move there, but Dad did not want to move us to France. He said the country was small and the chance for all of us to do well and better ourselves wouldn't be as good. Our family of ten was a normal size in Asia, but my dad realized that European families typically were smaller, and ten family members might be overwhelming for someone to sponsor. We never questioned him; whatever he said was fine, so we waited for a better opportunity.

Each family had many factors to consider when applying for their future dream homeland. I remember applications being sent to France, Australia, and Canada. My mom's first cousins could speak Chinese and Lao, so they applied to live in Hong Kong so that they would not have to learn another language. I think that having to learn a new language should not determine your destination for your permanent home. Instead, looking at the opportunities available there makes more sense. People were placed on a first come, first served waiting list based on their qualifications. Because my dad had worked for the government when the French ruled Laos, then he could have bumped to the front of the line to enter France. In fact, Dad was helping the families who wanted to go to France fill out their applications.

Also, due to my dad's extensive education, he had more knowledge about European countries and how they viewed immigrants. France was less likely to accept us as their own. Dad knew that the United States was much more accepting of other nationalities and also was a land of opportunity if you were willing to work. For this reason, Dad would not even consider applying for France, not wanting to take another family's spot on that waiting list. He was willing to wait it out in the refugee camp as long as it took to get the chance to enter the United States legally. This was our hope for a better, safer future.

The rumor around camp was that we could not go to America without a sponsorship. This made our large family feel we would have to wait longer for someone to agree to help us. Surprisingly, the opportunity to come to America was a bit easier than one might think. Someone from the United States would come to bring forms to fill out. The organization might have been UNICEF, but I am not exactly sure. When we filled out the forms, we stressed that we planned to work to better ourselves in our new country. That was natural for us, because Mom and Dad worked hard and valued education as a path to better lives. However, we knew our family was larger than most, and finding someone to sponsor a family of ten might take a while. Our family was willing to wait as long as it would take to be able to come to the United States, perhaps even until the refugee camp closed. If the camp, in fact, would have closed before we were granted permission to travel to America, Dad said he might consider Canada or Australia. So we were settled in, prepared for the long haul. Mom made many decisions about our family's future, but we all trusted Dad to decide where our new home would be. Dad's dream of our entire family living in the United States became our dream too.

Aunt Luckmany was the first family member to see her dream of moving to the United States come true. She was in the United

States at least a year before we came. When Aunt Luckmany was preparing to leave, we went into the city of Ubon to celebrate. I wore my red Adidas shirt, and Luckmany wore her yellow one (gifts from Aunt Tiane in France). I also had my impressive bell bottom slacks Mom brought for me from Laos.

One day in the summer of 1979, after more than two years in the camp, our dream was finally realized. There on the bulletin board, we saw our names listed to travel in July! We had about a month to get ready, and we were so excited to begin our new lives in the United States.

We had no idea who might be willing to help us get to America, but we really did not care. The only important thing was we were all together, and we were leaving the camp, headed to our new homeland.

chapter 12

The Journey to America

Once we knew for certain that we were going to America, our minds became focused on preparing to leave Southeast Asia for good. However, we still had responsibilities at the camp. Our home consisted of our ten family members plus my grandparents and two youngest uncles, for a total of fourteen mouths to feed. We had to continue providing for this group for another month, so Mom and I continued our farmers' market duties of buying and reselling. Today, as an adult, a month flies by quickly for me, but when I was eighteen, this month seemed to creep by. The anticipation of our new lives made it seem like the month would never end. As the time drew near for us to leave, we trained a relative to take over our marketing spot. We took her to town to introduce her to our suppliers and to show her the ropes on how to get around the area and where everything was. At the end of the month, we turned the business over to her. However, this relative did not keep the business going very long on her own. The experience Mom and I had gained over several years was hard to pick up in a single week.

We were not very sure of what to bring. Most of our knowledge of America was based on some European movies we had seen. These films showed many cold and snowy scenes with the actors wearing heavy coats, boots, and gloves, so we got the impression that it was always cold here. Of course, we had no heavy clothing, and we did not have money to buy many new supplies. Mom, however, was always thinking ahead. As soon as she realized that Dad had applied for America, she knew we would need warm clothes. Any time she could get her hands on some yarn, she would knit or crochet hats, scarves, sweaters (even turtleneck sweaters, which I could never stand to wear), and vests for all of us. In fact, I still have some of the items she made at the refugee camp.

We used some of our money to buy some new items. For example, my dad was adamant that we needed to buy a new rice steamer for his sticky or sweet rice, even though we were not even sure if we could purchase rice there. We kids were prepared to eat bread only, as most European movies showed people eating bread, not rice. Most of our camp utensils were going to stay there for my grandparents and uncles to use, including our rice steamer. The pots and pans were quite black and charcoal-coated from cooking over the campfires anyway, so we really did not want to pack those up to travel. One important item was our mortar and pestle. Every Asian cook used this to grind hot peppers, spices, and other food items. It was sort of like our man-powered food processor. These were usually clay and could break if dropped or pounded too hard. Mom took care of that worry by purchasing a cast-iron version to take with us. She even purchased a couple of different sizes of pots and pans to bring. Mom packed chopsticks, spoons, bowls, plates, and small hot sauce bowls. I remember we even brought an Asian machete, which would be quite difficult to bring through security in today's world. We brought all the dry goods Mom could think of, such as hot peppers and herbs. She could not imagine arriving in her new country without essential cooking items. Mom was always prepared, and if we were dropped off in the middle of the woods somewhere, she would still be able to put a meal in front of us.

We did not have enough suitcases for everything, just a couple of big ones. The older kids each carried a small duffle bag with a change of clothing, essentially the same as we had carried out of Laos two years before. We packed all the rest of our belongings we would take with us in heavy cardboard boxes we purchased from town. Any extra clothing was left behind for various friends and families who were in desperate need of such items.

The last few days in the camp were happy, exciting days. We visited with everyone, took lots of pictures (though I don't believe we ever saw those pictures), ate, and partied with many well-wishers. Whatever money Mom had left from her marketing budget was spent on food. Many people in the camp appreciated sharing in the great celebration feasts before we left.

Finally, the big day arrived! Two big buses arrived to take all the families whose names were on the list to travel that day. I assume most of these travelers were headed to America, but I do not really know for sure. After driving all day, we arrived in Lumphini Park in Bangkok, almost four hundred miles away. Apparently, the Thai government prepared this park as a holding area for those who were scheduled to fly out of the country at Suvarnabhumi International Airport, the biggest international airport in Thailand. Converting the park area to be used as a holding area was another indication of Thailand's generosity to help all these refugees. Thousands of refugees passed through this beautiful park, most certainly damaging the grounds and killing the plant life, while waiting to begin a new life. We were prepared to be there for up to a month, according to previous travelers' experiences. This park had a public bathroom with running water for restrooms and showers. Organizations provided hot meals in a soup kitchen fashion. The sleeping arrangements were in pavilions with roof and floor, but no sides, on a first come, first served basis. Windy rains would still soak you. Somehow, my mom had heard that we needed to bring mosquito nets with us so that we could sleep safely and also to set up the parameters of our space. We always had to have someone keep an eye on our items, so we placed them in the middle of our space, and at night, we slept around them. The mosquito netting was large enough to cover all ten of us and our belongings. Even during the day, we sat inside our mosquito nets. This kept the bugs off us all day, and we still enjoyed any breeze that blew through.

One might think this would be a stressful, anxiety-filled situation for our family to be stuck there in a park with hundreds of other refugees, but our family was not upset at all. We were still anticipating our brighter future, and we stayed alert, waiting for our next move. After a day or two, my parents figured out the routine. Families were not called to leave without warning; instead, they were alerted when their time was close and told that they should stay close and be prepared. The next morning, a bus would come to pick up the families who would have a chance to travel, and they would go to the airport. Once in a while, a family might not get on the planned flight, and they would return to spend another night at Lumphini Park with the plans to fly out the next day.

Mom had brought money to buy food for the family for up to a month at the park, as others had told her we might be there that long. Because food was provided by the soup kitchen, my parents used our food fund to take us out in a couple of taxis to a canal sightseeing area there in Bangkok. Dad remembered this area from when he stayed in Bangkok to study for three months a few years earlier. Even in this situation, Dad still wanted us to see and learn all we could while we were there. Dad believed that his ancestors helped dig this canal by hand during the time when Laos lost the war to Thailand, and we got to see it with our own eyes. After this outing, our extra money was depleted, so we stayed around the park until we were approved for traveling.

Up until this point, I had thought only Laos had suffered persecution and that all the refugees in our area would be from my homeland. To my surprise, I heard other languages spoken there at Lumphini Park as we awaited our turn to travel. I, like all my people, had been so naïve, not aware of the turmoil in so much of Southeast Asia. When Lao Issara took over, all broadcast and news reports were censored, so we were in the dark about much of what had been going on in our own country as well as in neighboring countries. Even if a citizen knew that something was going on, no one would speak out against our government at the risk of harsh punishment or even death. This was my first inkling that other countries also were suffering, many in much harsher circumstances than ours.

We were there about a week before we were called to fly out. As we picked up our belongings, Mom knew we would not need our mosquito nets anymore. She gave the netting to a family who was still there in the park without nets of their own. The only stipulation was that if we got bumped and had to return to the park for another night, we would get the nets back for our family's use until we left again.

At the airport, officials told us that anything we checked in would no longer be available to us until we arrived at our destination. Little did we know that our destination was our actual home address in Quincy, Illinois. We thought that was just another stop in our long journey. They slapped labels on all the boxes and suitcases and checked them in. That was the last we saw of the boxes until a couple of weeks later when they were delivered to Quincy.

From this point on, a man with a sign led all the refugees through the airport, not just our family. It was a fairly large group, with some who spoke a different language. We each carried a bag with personal items: a change of clothes, toothbrush, medicine, or whatever we might need until we got to our final destination. Each older sibling held a younger sibling's hand. Noi was a carry-on who we passed around as we traveled through the airport. We did not have tennis shoes for comfortable walking; we only had comfortable flip-flops or dressy shoes. Of course, I wanted to look my best, so I had chosen my high-heeled sandals, and this is what I had to wear as we walked what seemed like miles through the airport—not the best choice to wear as I carted my little brother around. Escalators were new to us, and Noi tried to take off while we were on one. Trying to hang on to him, I lost my balance, fell, and skinned my knees and elbows, all because I was a little overdressed for the occasion.

We did not really understand the procedures of refugees leaving, but looking back now, I realize we were all on a standby system. We were called to fill any open seats after the ticketed passengers had boarded. The jet was a huge Boeing 747 with four seats in the middle and two seats on each side of the rows. We did not all sit together, but we were all in the same general area, near the very back of the plane. We had a meal on the plane, but I do not remember another meal that evening.

We landed in Hong Kong, China, where we spent the night. We were transported from the airport there to some sort of a dormitory-type lodging with bunks on the walls, four high. We crawled in to sleep there for the night. The next morning a bus picked us up and took us to the airport, where we flew out again. I can't remember where or when we ate, but I do not remember being hungry, so someone had to feed us somewhere, maybe at the airport or on the airplane. Our connecting flight was through Tokyo, where we had a rather long layover in the Tokyo airport. The guides took us to a waiting area and had us stay there. I remember this was my first experience with an automatic toilet. I could not find a handle to flush it, but it flushed on its own. We all were confused. It was a lot to learn for a family who had not ever been exposed to such high-tech devices.

As we left the Tokyo airport, our group was getting smaller. Families were breaking off to go to different destinations. We arrived in Seattle and stayed there overnight. This time our lodging was more like a hotel. Our family had one room, and we spread out on the floor. Mom was worried about having no mosquito nets with us, but we figured out there were screens in the windows, so no bugs would have gotten in—such a pleasant freedom to just lie down anywhere! I don't believe we saw much in Seattle other than the airport. We had to travel between terminals, riding a sort of tram. This was new to us. Our family was treated to a meal in a nice restaurant at the Seattle airport, once again guided by a person with a sign. There was a buffet there on a rotating belt, and our guide tried to encourage us to pick out our food. We were overwhelmed by the American food options, such as hamburger, pizzas, hot dogs, and salad. We were looking for something recognizable like rice or stir-fry, but nothing looked familiar to us.

We had to watch how others ate, so we could follow their lead. Sing had a hamburger. We couldn't figure it out. Should he pick it up with his hands, or should he cut it up with a fork and knife to be proper? We were prepared for bread after our movie-watching experiences, but we did not know what a french fry was. Sing cut up his hamburger and took a bite, saying it had no flavor. I saw an American person with a hamburger who squirted packages of ketchup, mustard, or other condiments onto his burger. I told Sing to try that and to pick it up by hand, not cut it in pieces. He tried that and thought it didn't taste quite so plain. We were used to spicy, flavorful foods. The cook did all the seasoning; we did not have to add anything to the dish. As a matter of fact, it was considered rude to add to the dish unless the cook provided additional seasoning on the table. Asking for more spices meant that you felt the cook failed somehow. In Asia, we ate with spoons unless we had noodles, and then we used chopsticks. In the movies, we saw the characters eating with knives and forks and plates. In Asia, we did not need knives because the cook had already cut everything into bite-size pieces, and with limited meat available, we never had large pieces of meat anyway. We ate out of bowls of various sizes, but in America we were handed a plate. How would soup work on this? We were beginning to see just how much we had to learn.

We flew from Seattle to St. Louis, our final airport, where we finally met the first representative from our sponsors. An airport official met us as we walked off the plane and led us toward the baggage claim area. We were feeling a little lost and uncertain whether we were headed for another hotel or another connecting flight. However, we eventually saw a gentleman holding a big sign with "Sonethongkham" on it. Finally, someone was looking for us! Could this possibly be the final destination? We felt so relieved. This man seemed to be the angel my mom had been praying for to guide us to our new home. His name was named John French, the one who spearheaded our sponsorship and convinced his church to join him. We were certainly blessed by the First Presbyterian Church in Quincy, Illinois, under the ministry of Paul Beran. They definitely saw our need. They picked us because of our large family, thinking that perhaps few sponsors would be willing to work with such a large group.

John had our names on a list and the proper paperwork to prove he was legitimate. After papers were signed, the airport official let us go with him. John led us to the baggage claim area, but none of our checked bags and boxes came in. We followed John out of the airport to his lime-green Volkswagen van. That was before we had to wear seat belts, of course. He brought his son as well as his handicapped foster daughter in a wheelchair. There were thirteen of us in that one vehicle. I had two kids on top of me from St. Louis to Quincy. At this point, we were lucky that our checked items did not make it. Thank goodness! We would not have had room for it all.

When we crossed the Mississippi River, entering Illinois from Missouri, I remember my dad said, "We will have fishing!" Little did we know that we would be offered fishing and so much more.

chapter 13

Quincy

We had a wonderful community that opened their arms to us in Quincy. Many people worked and donated so we could have a wonderful new home. Although we didn't know what sort of lodging we would have, we had a house waiting for us on Lind Street, right across from Quincy College. We were surprised at this, and we each had our own bed! We had not had beds for so long, and these didn't even have mosquito nets, which was another surprise.

As soon as we got here, the church had a job waiting for my dad. It was at Speedrack, a steel manufacturing place. Mr. Bob Turner worked there, and he was the one who got Dad the job there. Mr. Turner took on the responsibility of showing my dad what to do because Dad knew very little English. Dad worked there until they laid him off. Then Dad worked for Sears on Twenty-Fourth Street until it closed. Then Sears transferred him to the mall location. He is Mr. Handyman, able to put together anything or keep it clean.

Though we did not know it at the time, Mr. and Mrs. Turner would be two of the most influential people to oversee our success there in Quincy. Not only did Mr. Turner ensure that my dad was successfully employed, but he and his wife, Margaret, helped my siblings and me as well. She helped tutor English and helped type any papers we needed to turn in. She read our lessons to us and tried to explain what was written. The first year we were here, several church members came to help tutor us in all of our subjects. The younger siblings, as they started grade school, received lots of help from various church members who volunteered to come read to them and help them with their English and other lessons. However, Bob and Margaret Turner tutored the older siblings through high school and college. We loved going to their home to study. Marge fixed all kinds of snacks that we did not have at home. Later on, our math and science lessons became more advanced, and Bob brought in an engineer from India who also worked at Speedrack to help us. Both of the Turners have passed now, but we will always be grateful to them for their love and support in getting us started here.

The first year we were in Quincy, several church members helped our family. Chris Nagle (formerly Chris Miles) went to nursing school and would come and chaperone us each day. John French would come to our home morning and night. He had hired my mom to babysit his kids after school. When he picked up his children, he would check on all of us to see if we needed anything at all. He did a sort of roll call, and if one of the kids would not be there, he would want to know where he was, who picked him up, who he was with, and so on. I realize now that he was tracking us closely to help keep us safe and on the right path. We could have so easily fallen into the wrong group and struggled in many ways.

When we started school, we kids didn't know English very well, so we had several church people come to tutor whatever subject they could help with. So there was lots of time and interest put into the kids' education. Another individual who stands out in my mind was Grandma Oakley, or Grace Oakley. She stopped by regularly to check in on us. No one ever said who provided the down payment for our home or the homes of two more families they sponsored; we were just told the church provided the down payments. I have every reason to believe that Grace Oakley might have had something to do with the loan. After Grace passed, my parents received notice that their loan was forgiven. This seems to be an indication that she was our benefactor.

Overall, though, the key figure who helped us achieve advanced academic success was Rick Smith. His wife, Bev, had earlier begun helping our family. In fact, when she learned that my dad was walking to work, her parents soon bought Dad a bicycle. Bev took a great interest in helping us any way she could, but sadly, she was stricken with cancer and passed away. Before she passed, she brought her husband, Rick, to our house a time or two. She was not feeling well, and she was only able to come by once in a while, bringing us various items. We were so sorry that we did not have more time with Bev, but her compassion for our family carried on through Rick. Rick worked at Quincy College in admissions, and his guidance ensured that the eldest children would, in fact, get a higher education.

After graduation, I wanted to be a nurse, and I took a course to become a nurse's aide. I could do the work as an aide, but the textbooks were too difficult for me to comprehend at that time. A nurse's aide job was supposed to be my way to make money while attending school to get an education. Rick came to my parents and presented a better way. He said that going to school and working at the same time would be too overwhelming for me. I needed to spend all my time with my classes. Rick said that he could get me scholarships that would pay for my schooling and provide additional money to help with my living expenses. If I lived at home, this could benefit the family. The one stipulation was that I had to carry a B average. With my language barrier, this would be an enormous challenge to achieve, but I was willing to try. I studied and studied, especially the classes that had lots of English and reading. I spent ten to fifteen hours a week on homework for that one three-hour class. I signed up for tutoring on any class that had lots of reading; I couldn't take notes well enough to prepare me for the tests. On the other hand, math, chemistry, and physics were no trouble at all.

I remember one proud memory from my Wednesday night class in logic. I did not have to take the final exam because I had scored so high on my regular tests. If only I did not have to take English composition or any literature classes, I would not have had to work quite so hard. Rick came through with his promises on funding, and I came through with hard work to keep my grades up. I earned a college degree in computer science with a minor in math and did not have to take out any student loans. Rick also helped my siblings get through college. Out of the eight children, Tay was the only one who did not attend at least two years of undergraduate work at Quincy College. Tay flip-flopped his education; he attended the University of Illinois for four years and then came back to get his master's degree at Quincy. Rick showed us the way, with the expectation that we had to do the hard work. Our family will be forever grateful for his services.

The Presbyterian Church saw how their sponsorship had touched our lives and helped us to become successful, and they wanted to continue their mission by helping another family. They pleasantly surprised us by sponsoring the Sengmany family from Laos, the second family sponsored by the church. The church could have sponsored a family from Cambodia or Myanmar, or they might have sponsored Laotians from a different area, such as Hmong in Laos, who spoke quite a different dialect from us. However, the Sengmany family spoke our dialect and could easily communicate with us. The church was aware of our family's isolation there in Quincy and wanted to bring over a family who could offer us a sense of community.

After this, my parents realized that the church was willing to sponsor more families to come to Quincy, so Mom began to work on Mr. Turner to see if he would be able to help bring Grandpa Song, Grandma Houay, Uncle Soutchay, and my baby uncle Khamla. My grandparents and uncles were not able to travel with us to the United States because the paperwork was only for the ten of us, so they had stayed in our hutch at the camp in Thailand. Mr. Turner could not tell her no, and our family in Quincy grew. Bob and Margaret Turner, with the First Presbyterian Church cosigning, sponsored these four family members to come to America, where they joined us in 1980. They lived with us for a while until they could get their own place.

Dave Little and his former wife, Laura Doran, also helped us; they are still like parents to us. Dave was a lawyer, and Mom would take every letter to him to read, paying him with egg rolls. Mom got to know Dave and Laura fairly well, and she felt comfortable enough to ask them for help in sponsoring her brother Seng and his family to come to Quincy. Whether or not they wanted to help, Mr. Dave could not tell her no. My mom was unrelenting in her sweet talk and pleading, and her egg rolls finished the deal. Even now when we see Dave, he reminds us how persistent Mom was, saying, "Please, Mr. Dave!" Uncle Seng was the last of Mom's family to come to Quincy.

Our next-door neighbor, Linda Hibbert, was not a member of the church, but she really looked out for us. If anything looked out of place, or if she saw a need at all, she would call someone from the church to let them know. She had three boys who were friends with Noi, and I helped her at times by babysitting her boys.

The youngest ones learned English faster, and so they adapted faster. You learn more quickly when you are younger. Noi, as the youngest, considers English as his first language and Lao as his second. He never did master the Lao language and thinks in English rather than in Lao. I am probably the worst with English. It was hard for me. At first, I knew just two words: yes and no. I don't know how I learned English other than I really loved to talk, so I kept trying and letting people correct me. Nobody can teach you a language until you have the intent to learn. Then you figure it out. Everyone always laughs at the way I say things backward, but they usually know what I mean.

Sing and I wore out the Lao/English and Thai/English dictionaries the first two or three years. The Thai/English dictionary was more complete and thus more helpful to us. The Lao/English could only translate the most basic words, so when we needed more complex words and terms, we needed to go to the Thai/English one. I think that probably this is because Thailand was an English colony, while Laos was a French colony. At first, I tried to look up every word, but each word would have so many meanings. I might spend twenty minutes on one sentence. It took me forever!

When we were learning English, oddly enough, we started simply from a couple of friends going to the library to get baby books. Fortunately, we had taken a little French, so we could sound words out better. I don't really know how I learned English, maybe partly from watching TV. We didn't have any other Laotian families around at first, so we had to speak English to anyone outside our home. We got paid for going to an English learning program called CITA. Mom was excited because we could all go, and we actually got paid to attend. Mom got a check for grocery money, so she made our attendance a priority. These classes did, indeed, help us. The material was presented more at our own level rather than how the English courses at school presented the material.

Because a church had sponsored us, we had lots of church activities to attend, and each activity offered us more practice for our English learning. People from our new church would come and pick us up every Sunday morning for church, and they also brought us to other activities throughout the week. We did not ever miss any of these activities. We couldn't back out; Asians are very polite and wouldn't want to hurt anyone's feelings. We came to youth group. We couldn't talk on the phone to cancel; we would just be ready to go whenever they came. At the first Easter egg hunt at the church, I remember it was fun to take Noi out and pick up candy. We all enjoyed the sugary treats. Church members took us to several fun youth group outings. The first Illinois farm we visited was the Warren and Shirley Speckhart farm near Payson. I was not aware that we were so close to rural areas, as we lived in what we considered the big city of Quincy. I remember petting their horse and swimming in their creek. Our first hayride was a totally new experience for us. We were in awe at the huge fields of corn that covered acres and acres of farmland; we had never seen anyone plant so much corn. The only corn we had ever seen grew in gardens for people to consume; we had not seen field corn before. Soybeans were new to us. The only beans we knew were yard beans, which were green pole beans that we ate.

One church family worked especially hard to help us fit in and to give us enjoyable experiences there in Quincy. John and Betsy Owens had five children of their own, yet they made time for our family. They owned a boat, but not a fishing boat like Dad was used to; it was more of a pleasure boat. When we crossed the Mississippi River to live in Quincy, Dad had envisioned that he would be fishing there, but he really did not have a boat of his own and had to rely on others to take him. John fished, but mostly on ponds or off the dam on the south side of Quincy, and he sometimes took Dad with him. However, I remember the time John and his family took us out for a day of boating on the Mississippi River. We picnicked on a sandbar and had so much fun. But I did encounter a not-so-enjoyable experience. As Asians, we usually tried to stay out of the sun; we preferred our skin tone to be as light as possible. After our day of boating with the Owens family, I had the worst sunburn I ever had experienced, severe enough that my skin peeled. I believe their family was applying sunscreen, and I am sure they offered it to me, but I did not really know what it was or why I might need it. I certainly learned a lesson there!

Dawn Owens, John and Betsy's eldest daughter, became a very good friend and one of the most helpful contacts for me in high school. She was a bright student and took it upon herself to escort Sing and me around our large school, Quincy Senior High 2. She would walk with us to our class and then be there for us afterward to get us to the next class. Sing and I signed up for exactly the same schedule so we could help each other; fortunately, Dawn was also enrolled in our American history class. She took notes for us and helped us study, getting us through the class successfully. Lunchtime can be one of the most awkward times for new kids who spoke differently, but Dawn sat with us as we ate. Sometimes the smallest gestures can make the biggest differences for others. When we were trying to learn English, Dawn was the one who took us to the library to read the baby books for practice.

Dawn and another friend, Judy Johnson Huss, along with Bill Echelbarger and Todd Still, always found us at Youth Group, making us feel welcome and helping us to fit in as well as we could, even though we did not understand much of what anyone was saying. I recall one time when Chris Miles Nagle was at our house and someone knocked on our door. Chris answered the door for us, and it was Bill and Todd. I could not really understand what they were saying, but I caught on that they were asking me to go somewhere with them. I immediately said no, not wanting to commit to anything I did not understand. I found out later that they had just asked me to come to the backyard to play some sort of game with them and my brothers, a rather harmless request. I always considered Bill and Todd to be Sing, Ott, and Tay's friends—boys who were just a little younger and who hung out with my brothers quite a bit. They were great at helping my brothers out, especially in social situations like youth group. However, years later, I connected with Todd on Facebook, and he revealed to me that apparently I had more of an effect on him. In his Facebook message, he apologized to me for being so awkward in his younger years, not himself by any means. He said that he thought I was so pretty that I made him nervous and shaky. It sounds a little bit like a crush that totally escaped my notice.

Pastor Paul Beran's eldest daughter, Monica Beran Koehn, and Janet Speckhart Janssen (Warren and Shirley Speckhart's daughter) were also good friends who visited our family often and still remain good friends today. Pastor Beran and his family hosted us in their home on occasion. One time in particular that stands out was a winter wiener roast in the basement fireplace, a fun time for sure. The Berans were gracious church leaders who did not stand in the way of our sponsorship, but instead, encouraged church members to include us and support us in various activities.

The kindness and help shown to us by members of First Presbyterian Church definitely made our new experiences easier. For many other experiences, trial and error was our approach. For example, we had to experiment a bit to figure out our food supply. My mom had a garden right away in the backyard, using some of the seeds she brought with her. The first year of our garden, someone gave Mom zucchini seeds, which was a new crop for us. Mom let the zucchini get really large so one of the vegetables would feed more mouths, even though a larger zucchini is not quite as tasty as a smaller one. The first year we did not preserve anything from our garden. We did not know how to go about preserving food for the winter. This was our first real winter, and Mom was very disappointed when the first frost killed all of her garden. That winter was when Mom realized that buying fresh fruits and vegetables was about as expensive as buying meat such as a whole chicken or a whole ham on a hog. Suddenly, our diet became more meat than vegetables. Mom was not familiar with canned or frozen vegetables, so she was not aware that these would have been a cheaper way to go. We survived on rice and meat with very small amounts of vegetables added. This was a real change in our diet, but we kids actually thought it was a pretty tasty change. The whole winter, Mom was counting the days until she could plant her garden. She asked Mr. French every day if it was time for garden, and he would laugh and tell her, "No, not yet, Bouany!"

The first snow was quite a memorable event for us. We had only seen snow in movies, and we did not realize it was so cold when we sprinted outside barefoot to catch snow on our tongues. Back in Laos, we never wore socks. The first year we really struggled when we had to put on socks. I used to pull my socks off as soon as I came home. We had never even worn closed-toed shoes. Coats and gloves were new attire for us. It was quite obvious that we didn't know how to dress for winter. Because we didn't have any boots, I believe our sponsor might have paid for boots for us, all from Payless ShoeSource. People would go out of their way to make our lives better.

CITA was not the only way we could make extra money. The second summer we were in Quincy, we became strawberry pickers. Someone from the church knew of a strawberry patch owner named Pete Holschlag who would pay for someone to pick strawberries for him. Pete's nephew came to pick us up. All eight of us kids piled in a car to go pick strawberries. We did not have a clue what a strawberry was, but we were happy to do whatever we could do to be outside and to earn a little money. We were very trusting to go with anyone who came to pick us up, given that we couldn't communicate. The first day we went, each of us brought home some cash from our efforts. Mom saw this and thought she might be able to go pick strawberries too. We kids didn't want her to come out in the sun, working a back-straining job, so we wanted to protect her. The only way we knew to keep her home was to tell a little white lie. We told her the strawberry trees were too tall for her to reach, and this kept her home the first year. This was the first job where all the kids could work and bring home cash to contribute to the family. Eventually, Mom had a nice bundle of our earnings saved up, and we kids thought it might be nice for her to have a freezer to preserve her garden harvest. We approached John French about purchasing a freezer for Mom, and he took Sing, Ott, and me to buy one. We were so proud to buy such a big item with our money. We did not buy the largest size; we couldn't imagine Mom filling it up. (We were so wrong on this. She needed the biggest one there with all her garden produce and later on meat from the Kurfman farms.) However, this medium-sized freezer was such a godsend for our family, and in fact, it still works great to this day.

When I was a young girl, in some ways, I was spoiled; I didn't have to do any cooking or housecleaning. We had someone living with us. We were not rich, but help was very reasonable, so I did not have many household duties until I was high school age. That was when I had to be responsible for money to spend for food. I never knew how to cook until I came to the United States. Even in Thailand, my mom and I came to town to get items for the market, and my grandma would cook for us and bring it to us. Suddenly, in the United States,. I had to learn to wash and clean, and I managed to fix a few types of food to keep the kids' bellies full while Mom was caring for the little ones. But I was usually cleaning the kitchen, refrigerator, and so on. Washing was something my mom allowed me to be responsible for more and more.

When I got married, my mother-in-law was in Home Extension, and I learned more about canning and freezing and other ways to prepare food. I had always loved gardening, but I didn't know how to cook so much. As a housewife in America, I learned how to cook and serve two types of food at the same time. When I was hungry for Asian food, I cooked that, but my poor husband had to eat too. I had to try to find something I could fix for him. He was so hungry for hamburger, but in Asia my mom never cooked hamburger. I decided that was one of the first things I had to learn to prepare. I started out with spaghetti because I could prepare noodles fairly well. Over the years, my cooking has evolved into a fusion of Asian and American cuisine. Our kids always had to have rice to go with our meal. Carl does not like rice, so I always tried to have green beans for him. I also love to grill various foods, even though my mom never grilled. I am thankful that many people patiently taught me and the rest of my family how to cook along with how to manage our household. It's kind of like instead of handing people fish to eat, you must teach them to fish so they will have food for a lifetime. Caring individuals taught us how to fish, so to speak, by showing us how to get by in our new home.

I learned many other skills here. For the first year, Chris Miles Nagel brought our groceries all the time, but eventually, I was able to take over some transportation duties. I had never driven at all in Laos, so learning to drive was something entirely new to me. My mom didn't have a car, but my dad had a car and a driver's license. My brother Sing learned how to drive, but he got a little cocky about when and where he would drive, only driving if it fit his schedule. Mom said maybe I should learn to drive. However, it was kind of hard to get driving practice time with just one car. I just studied the rules and did not drive the highway. Eventually, I got my license and I could help get groceries and drive Mom places. Mom had a license in Laos, but she did not have one to drive here in Illinois. Even though she was a good driver, the language barrier made it hard to take the written test. Eventually, though, she did get her license to drive.

When we first came to America, we each had to have a green card with our own number on it, so we would be legal to stay here. The application process took two years. We were interviewed more than once while we were in the camp, probably to provide missing information about our family. I recall at one of the interviews we had a health screening, with someone looking into our mouths and checking our teeth for decay. We really did not know exactly what information they needed; we had to trust that the people working with our sponsors were taking care of the details. Having green cards would allow us to live and work permanently in the United States. Once we settled into our new home in Quincy, we took our cards to apply for Social Security numbers so that we could work and pay taxes.

A few years later, our family members wanted to become official citizens. The United States offered only two ways to become a citizen, either by birth or by choice. Obviously, we were not born here, so each of us chose to become a naturalized citizen. After we had lived here for about eight years, my parents, some of my older siblings, and I were the first ones to apply. We had to learn about the country's government and show basic English skills. I remember they asked Mom to speak something in English, and I told her this. I asked her to tell them what color the sky was in English, and she said, "The sky is blue." That was enough for them. We all passed our interviews. We later participated in an Immigration and Naturalization Service ceremony in Springfield, where a courtroom full of new citizens took an oath to protect the Constitution. We were official citizens with all the rights, including the right to vote, the right to help protect our country by bearing arms, and the right to serve in any elected office except the presidency.

What a long, winding journey we had taken to come from our tiny, chaotic homeland of Laos to becoming official US citizens! This proves that knowledge, perseverance, and careful planning can provide opportunities to those who set goals and work to achieve them.

chapter 14

Saying "I Do" to Carl

Our family was the first Laotian family to settle in Quincy. The local paper, the *Quincy Herald-Whig*, published an article about how well my siblings and I were doing in school, despite the language barrier and cultural differences. This article most likely sparked an interest for other churches and organizations to also sponsor refugees. One tiny church about thirty-five miles from Quincy felt led to sponsor a Laotian family. A few months after we moved here, some members from Fishhook United Brethren Church came to our home and asked if one of us would go with them when they met the family as they arrived at the Quincy airport. My brother Sing agreed to go to help with the communication barrier. My brother was not fluent in English, but he could offer some reassurance to the Sabengsy family, helping them realize that they would not be totally isolated from their Lao culture. The Sabengsys became close friends of our family. Sounthone, the mother, had lived fairly close to where our family lived back in Laos. She had heard of my parents. She and Bounhome had two boys, Keokaysone, who was about four or five years old, and Viloath, a newborn. This family lived in a house near Neal and Margaret Jo Kurfman, on a farm the Kurfmans farmed, and they came to our home nearly every weekend, enjoying the comfort of fellowship with other Laotians.

The Sabengsys introduced my family to Neal and Margaret Jo, my future in-laws. These two were instrumental in their church's sponsorship of the Sabengsys to come to America, and they continued to support and mentor the family. One day Neal approached me to see if I would consider babysitting Keokaysone and Viloath while their parents took classes at Quincy College to learn English as a second language. I would have gladly watched the boys without compensation; they were like part of the family and were at our house quite frequently. However, Neal insisted that he would pay me. Neal and Margaret Jo would make a point to stop in. Apparently, he had an ulterior motive. He had an unmarried son, and Neal was beginning to think that I might be a good fit as his daughter-in-law. He teased me, telling me he had someone for me to meet. Straightforward persistence was Neal's nature, but he always softened it with his teasing and sense of humor. For example, when he was in the hospital, he would put pictures of Carl and Carl's cousin Kevin on the wall and try to play matchmaker with every available nurse who came in.

My dad started to go to visit Bounhome and Sounthone's home on the farm. Dad and Bounhome would hunt on the Kurfmans' farm property. Neal was very generous to Dad and our family, giving beef or pork when he butchered. Even if we asked to buy a hog, Neal and Margaret Jo would never accept the full price. I wonder if this was all meant to soften my dad so that he would consider Carl as his potential son-in-law. Our culture did not actually arrange marriages, but the parents had a huge influence on who their children would marry, so all of Neal's kindness might have helped with the matchmaking, at least to some extent.

As time passed, Mom and Dad would visit the Sabengsys

at the farm, maybe for the day, or maybe to stay overnight, and sometimes even my younger siblings might get to tag along. But I always stayed home with the rest of the kids to monitor homework, cook meals, and watch after them, so the rest of my family knew the farm and the Kurfman family before I did. Neal would take them hunting morel mushrooms in the spring, and Nang absolutely loved to go mushroom hunting with Neal. I, on the other hand, had no idea how to hunt mushrooms or deer or anything else; I just stayed at our home in Quincy and babysat the kids left behind.

After a few more Lao refugee families were sponsored and moved into the area, the First Presbyterian Church and the Fishhook UB Church wanted to create an opportunity for all the refugees and their sponsors to meet. A public rest area near Fishhook had picnic facilities and restrooms, so the two churches planned a picnic there. This is the event where Carl and I first met. My poor English prevented me from conversing much with Carl, but at least I knew what he looked like. After that, every time the Sabengsys would come to my house, they would say, "Carl said to say hello." I would smile and tell them to say hi for me too.

One time I drove Mom and Dad to the Kurfmans' farm to butcher a hog, and when I got there, Carl offered for our family to take some corn from the field. Field corn is not quite as tasty as sweet corn, but it is actually pretty good if you pick it at just the right time, before it gets too big. Carl asked me to ride along with him to get the corn. I told Mom in Laotian that if she wanted corn, she would have to go with me. I wasn't going to ride alone with him to the field, so Mom hopped in too. I don't think that was in Carl's plan.

I have to chuckle now when I look back on that day. I knew Carl was interested in me, but I did not know for sure if farm life would be for me. Even though I had lived in some tiny communities in Laos in addition to my homes in urban areas, I did not grow up around agriculture. My younger years were spent in school, buying and selling for the business, or taking care of my siblings. I liked planting flowers and a vegetable garden, but I did not really know much about crops and livestock. Neal and Margaret Jo seemed nice. Carl seemed nice, but I really did not want to lead him on when I was not sure that I could handle living on a farm. However, Neal, with his persistent nature, kept the idea of a future marriage alive. I remember one time he told me that Carl was scheduled to go to Hawaii on an agriculture-related trip, and Neal asked me if I would like to go along. I was horrified! No decent, unmarried Asian girl would consider taking a trip with a man. So I turned down a free trip to Hawaii, keeping my distance from Carl at that point.

The friendship between the Kurfman family and my family grew. Neal often found ways to spend time with us, even in unlikely situations. For example, Neal was a little bit accident-prone, and he occasionally would end up in the hospital as a result of some mishap, usually something do to with his three-wheeler ATV. While he was biding his time as a patient, Neal would usually call our house, hoping for visitors, especially hoping that I might stop by with my parents to see him. Neal had a deep connection with the Sabengsys, almost like adopted family to him, and this, in turn, kept him connected with us. All of us were just as close to the Sabengsys, offering support in any way we could. The Kurfmans and Sonethongkhams together provided Laotian as well as American support for the Sabengsys in their new environment.

Our family faced a challenge in the summer of 1982, when I had just finished my sophomore year at Quincy College. We rented our home from Quincy College, and that summer the college decided they wanted the house back to use for student housing. We had to find somewhere else to live. With such a large family, supported only by my dad's income, this was a predicament. The houses in our price range were far too small for all of us. We were essentially homeless. Part of our family stayed with Uncle Seng, and the older children went to stay with the Turners. This is where we often went for homework help anyway, and they were sort of like our American parents. We were hoping to find a place to live before school started, but it was not an easy task.

Neal and Margaret Jo learned of our situation from the Sabengsys, and they were determined to help us. They came to my parents and invited them to look at an empty farmhouse that belonged to Carl. If Mom and Dad thought it would be suitable, we were welcome to stay there as long as we needed to without charge. My parents were very thankful and accepted the offer. Carl would not accept rent from us, and he even paid for our electricity and water. Even though we did not have air conditioning, we were very grateful to have shelter at no cost. Dad drove to Quincy each day to his job at Sears.

I did not move into this house with them at the time. Sing and I stayed in Quincy at the Turners' because we both had jobs on cleaning crews at the college through the work study program. As this setup continued, I could sense that Mom and Dad were feeling a little sad and stressed from not having our own place to live and from not having us all under the same roof. I could not magically produce a new home for us, but I wanted to try to brighten their spirits somehow. I thought it might help if I would move to the farm with them and then begin to commute to Quincy with Dad. The goal was to try to cheer them up a little and spend more family time with the young ones. Sing, however, continued living with the Turners for the summer.

My decision to stay at the farm for those few weeks that

summer was a turning point for me. I realized that staying out in the country was not as hard as I thought. It was peaceful, quiet, and not nearly as lonely as I thought it would be. Even though my parents had repeatedly told me that Carl came from a good family, I had not given Carl much of a chance to get to know me, but Mom saw Carl every day and appreciated him. Each day, while Dad and I were in Quincy, Carl would come to the farmhouse to check on Mom and the little ones who were there with no car. Carl would bring garden produce or other goodies from his parents and make sure Mom was okay.

Neal knew that in order for my parents to start renting a new place, they would need a deposit of at least two months' rent. Dad, Sing, and I already received paychecks, and to supplement this income, Neal found work for Ott, Tay, and Nang detasseling corn for Burrus Seed Farms. The boys drove a little green Pinto that Mr. Turner had sold to our family. That poor car could barely pull itself up a hill, but it got the detasseling crew to the bus on time. Carl also provided an additional paycheck for Ott and Tay by hiring them to help put up hay on the farm. Tay was driving the tractor once and nearly killed Carl when his shifting was so jerky that all the bales fell off the trailer, taking Carl with them. Luckily, he survived the experience.

During our summer of staying on the farm, Carl cleverly devised a plan to get to closer to me. During the day, he would tell the kids about some sort of fun, local activity in the evening that they might enjoy. Of course, he told them that their big sister needed to come along to help chaperone. When I would get home from work, the kids would beg for me to go so Carl would take them. These trips to the fair, roller skating, and even Six Flags amusement park in St. Louis provided so many wonderful memories for my younger siblings. It was as if all seven of us were dating Carl. He had to pay for everything from the gas he used to all the food we ate to the admission tickets at each event. Our family had no spare money to help. Carl and I did not go anywhere with just the two of us that summer; instead, he took a gang of Sonethongkhams. In my mind, I assumed as soon as our family found a place in Quincy, Carl and I would probably drift apart. I viewed myself as no more than a homeless refugee girl with seven siblings to tend to. Who would want to take on this sort of responsibility? I thought that spending so much money on my crew all summer long would probably scare anyone away. But not the Kurfmans.

That summer revealed what type of man Carl Kurfman is. I appreciated his kindness and generosity. He was very shy, but he had such a good heart. He saw value in me that I did not even realize on my own. Though our differences were many, including culture, language, food, religion, and so on, I began to look at him differently, as if he could possibly be a prospect after all. As a young refugee woman, I knew I brought a lot of baggage into a relationship, but he overlooked all that. Another factor in his favor was that his parents were so kind to me and my family. I appreciated that their family did not look down on any of us in our struggles here. We were at our lowest point—homeless and uncertain of our future living situation—and their compassion and willingness to help meant so much to me.

The Kurfmans were not the only ones who were looking out for us that summer. We had no idea at the time, but our First Presbyterian sponsors were working behind the scenes to find a home for our family. Mr. Dave Little was one of the primary figures who helped find and acquire a new home for us. He was a lawyer who learned of a two-story house near Quincy College that was going through foreclosure. The church financed a down payment and took care of the details to secure this home for my family. Just before school started, we had a home, and we could continue attending our same school district. The payments were within our budget and very close to the amount of our previous rent, but now we would be investing in a home that we would one day own. Such a blessing!

My family was back in Quincy, only a couple of blocks from the college. I could walk to work at the college cafeteria and to campus to attend classes as I began my junior year. After dating my whole family for the summer, Carl began to come to Quincy on Friday evenings to take me out, but our dating was not exactly like most other young couples. I was waiting tables at the China Inn on Friday and Saturday nights. Carl had given me his car to drive so I could get back and forth to this job, and he would drive his truck to Quincy to take me out to eat after my Friday night shift. If I was later coming home from work, Carl would just hang out at my house. Often, I would come home, and Noi would be on his lap, asking all his "Why?" questions. With my busy school and work schedule, this was our one date night I allotted to spend time alone with Carl. Sunday was another time we spent together when I came to church at Fishhook, but that probably would not be considered an actual date. This was before cell phones, texting, or email, and we did not really chat much on the phone in between either. With a family of ten, our home phone was not for socializing but just for quick calls for information. Even though we did not interact every day or spend hours on the phone, now I could officially call Carl my boyfriend. By Christmas of 1982, we were engaged.

Because we were blending two worlds, my traditional Lao culture and modern American culture, we knew that our wedding would be somewhat challenging to pull off, so we had to compromise in a few areas. For example, in order for a Lao boy to obtain permission to marry, an elder from his family would go to his bride's parents or to other relatives if the elder did not feel close enough to her parents. The elders and her relatives would discuss the suitability of the marriage proposal and agree on the dowry. The larger the dowry, the better the tribute to the bride and her family, as well as a sign of the groom's family's financial success. If the bride's family did not have much wealth, that dowry could be used to help pay for the wedding and feast that came with it. If the bride's family was financially secure, the dowry might be gifted to the newlyweds.

The engagement in Laos is a commitment, and if the groom breaks the engagement for any reason, he would most likely be fined, usually at least double the agreed-upon dowry price. The day of the elder asking for the girl's parents' permission was like an engagement party, with extended family invited to a big feast. However, we skipped this step and opted for a more American procedure. Carl asked me if I wanted to marry him, and I said yes. We picked out a ring, and then we went to my family to share our news. My parents, of course, were anticipating a dowry, but I set them straight. "We are in America … Don't expect a dowry. It would look like you're selling your daughter!"

We began plans for our wedding. Carl and I wanted to marry the next summer, but I still had another year of college to complete. Education was an extremely high priority for Dad; he was adamant that I should not allow anything to get in the way of my degree, and he preferred that we wait a year before our marriage. (Carl's parents, however, did not want to see us wait another year. They were very impatient for their son to marry and begin to provide the grandbabies they had been so anxious to see!) Carl had to promise Dad that I would finish my classes and obtain my degree, and I helped Carl keep his word when I received my degree in 1984. My dad should not have ever worried about this; I was driven by my own determination to finish my schooling.

I wanted to be able to take care of myself in case an unforeseen need would arise.

Another even larger problem was how to pay for the wedding. Tradition in both Laos and America was that the bride's parents usually paid for the wedding, which was a real predicament for me because my parents did not have any extra money to pay for such an expense. This is where my future in-laws came to the rescue. Neal and Margaret Jo offered to pay for the entire wedding. This included my dress, my mom's dress, my sister's dress, and all the tuxedo rentals for any of my family members who were in the wedding, including my dad, brothers, and uncles. They also paid for the flowers, cake, and everything else. We had a fairly large wedding with all our family members invited. Guests were served punch, cake, and hors d'oeuvres at the church. However, we did not have a large reception afterward for a couple of reasons. One reason was that Neal and Margaret Jo were paying for so much already. I did not want to add on the cost of another festivity with music, food, and dancing. Another reason was that Carl was very, very nervous about the possibility of dancing in front of everyone. A reception did not matter to me, so we skipped it and saved the Kurfmans some expense.

Looking back now, I think I perhaps my in-laws had another reason for paying for the wedding. They may have been worried that I would back out on Carl. I was not a typical young girl who was dependent on seeing my boyfriend all the time. Instead, I was comfortable with our weekly dates and did not call or demand attention in between. Neal, in particular, may have worried that I was losing interest, but he did not know me. I have always been a person of my word, and when my mind is made up, I follow through. When I said I would marry Carl, I meant it. I just happened to be a rather busy and independent young woman who was comfortable whether we were together or apart.

Planning a wedding in America proved to be a challenge for me and for some of Carl's family members. When Carl's only girl cousin, Kathy Henthorn Dyer, took me shopping for my wedding dress, we definitely had some English barrier problems. While we were looking at all the dresses, I said, "I want a tail on my dress."

Kathy told me, "No, that's a train."

I said, "You mean 'woo woo, choo choo'?"

Kathy explained that the train on a wedding dress is the longer part that trails behind on the floor. Then at the tux store, I said that I wanted Carl to wear a white jacket with a train. Kathy told me that was a tail. I am sure I looked exasperated as I threw up my hands. One more crazy twist to learning English!

On the morning of July 9, 1983, we held a traditional Lao ceremony in my parents' home. Then later that day, we were married in the First Presbyterian Church in Quincy with our families and friends there to support us. Carl and I were united that day, but we were not the only ones. Two families from completely different backgrounds were united when we were married, and over the years, we have learned from one another, helped each other, and, overall, have been very blessed. Rev. Clifford Phillips helped perform the ceremony. Coincidentally, Clifford resigned the next day as the pastor at Fishhook. A young minister was asked to fill in until we could find a permanent pastor. Rev. Mark Dickerson was hired as the temporary fill-in who continues as the Fishhook U.B. Church pastor to this day. He and his wife, Cheryl, have unselfishly served our church and our community for more than three decades.

Our honeymoon was a road trip to see more of the country I now called home. The first night, though, we did not plan to travel too far; we had a reservation in a hotel in Hannibal for the first night of our trip, or at least we thought we did. A few weeks earlier, we were in Hannibal, and Carl decided to reserve a room at a hotel there for the first night after the wedding, so he parked at that hotel but told me to stay in the car and he would handle everything. He went on inside and reserved the honeymoon suite there. After the wedding ceremony was finished, all the pictures were taken, and refreshments were served, we headed to Hannibal. As we attempted to check in at the hotel desk, we encountered a problem. They did not have a record of our reservation. Instead of the honeymoon suite, we had a regular room, but I suppose we were fortunate to have any sort of room at all. Every once in a while I remind Carl that he still owes me a honeymoon suite stay.

The next day we set out on a journey full of new sights and experiences. Since I had come to Quincy to live, the only places I had traveled to were Fishhook, the Kurfman farm, and then occasional trips with my family to visit Dad's distant relatives in Elgin, Illinois. Carl and I left Hannibal and started driving, and one of the first stops was a Civil War cemetery in Vicksburg, Mississippi. Carl has always enjoyed history, and he still takes any opportunity to see historical sites when we travel. I had studied the Civil War in my American history class, but I really did not really understand what I was seeing in Vicksburg until I read up on it later. Still, I enjoyed the different monuments there.

We continued on to New Orleans, and without cell phones, finding lodging in the downtown area took some time and effort because we had to stop at a hotel, walk in, and ask in person if there was a room available. We were not having any luck. The one-way streets were narrow and difficult to navigate, but we kept pressing on. We really did not get to see the French Quarter except from our car as we searched for a hotel. I saw many stands with vendors selling various goods, such as bundles of hanging garlic and onions, and I thought that Mom and I could probably find success there.

Continuing through the city, meandering through those

crowded streets, we had to wait on a drawbridge to be raised for a boat to go through. I had never seen a bridge open up like that. As we waited for the bridge to close again, I was struck by the beauty of the old oak trees draped with Spanish moss. We finally found an available room in a hotel just outside the city limits. Though we did not actually tour the heart of New Orleans that evening, at least we had a place to stay, and it even had a pool. Carl does not enjoy water, but I have always loved to swim. That evening I was enjoying swimming in our hotel pool while Carl relaxed nearby in one of the pool chairs, when I noticed a woman hanging around Carl, talking to him. He looked a little uncomfortable and eventually motioned to me that he was ready to leave. He told me she was a woman truck driver who was flirting with him and trying to pick him up. He had pointed to me and said he was married, but he could not get her to leave. I laughed and told him that the girls were all after him now that he was wearing a wedding ring.

The next morning, we were checking out to leave, and several people were in the lobby with lots of commotion. I poked Carl to ask what was going on, so he checked it out. It was a tour group about to get on a bus for a tour of New Orleans. We asked if they had room for two more, and they did, so we put our bags in our car and joined the tour, which ended up being a great idea. We saw several city sights, a port where huge ships sailed out, and plantations that had huge homes with slave quarters. When we stopped for a lunch break, I remember another couple a bit older than we were who caught my attention. The man kept calling his wife baby doll, which I found rather amusing. Because of my strict Asian background, I was more reserved. We did not really show much public affection, so this older couple probably looked more like the newlyweds of the group.

After the tour ended, the bus took us back to our car, and we set out again, headed toward Tampa. At one point, Carl asked me to figure out which lane he needed to get in. I looked at him and said, "Which direction are you going?" North, east, south, and west never did mean much to me. He handed me the map and I turned it the way we were going to try to figure out where we needed to be. Carl quickly discovered that I had never used a map before; Sing and Ott were the map readers to help Dad drive to Elgin. After I began to get the hang of it, I could help Carl pretty well. This trip was my crash course in map reading.

We drove on to Florida, where we visited Disney World, Epcot Center, Busch Gardens in Tampa, and Cypress Gardens before heading back home. For a girl who had never been anywhere before, our honeymoon was quite an experience. I am so glad that Carl developed a love of traveling as a young boy vacationing with his parents. The Kurfmans would often travel with another family from the Fishhook church, Marvin and Leah Mabel Hull and their two daughters, Peggy and Susan. The two families were very close, and we even have a picture of Carl as a little boy down on one knee, looking like he was proposing to Susan. Susan became a very close friend to me before she lost her battle with cancer a few years ago, and she used to joke about this. Once in a while she would say, "Carl took me on a trip to _____. Did he take you there?" Carl did not realize at the time when he pulled off such a wonderful trip for our honeymoon that he was creating a monster obsessed with traveling. In our years of marriage, we have traveled to every state and several other countries. I am like a little kid in a candy store, wanting to go anywhere, anytime.

After we returned home, I moved to the farm to begin the next stage of my life as a farmer's wife.

chapter 15

The Life of a Farm Wife

When I was dating Carl, I did not know much about farming. I knew a few items of machinery, such as a tractor, and I knew that a pig was a farm animal, but I could not name specifics. I did not know then that a mommy pig is a sow, a baby pig is a piglet, or that a daddy pig is a boar. The same went for cows. However, I was a quick learner.

My earlier refugee camp experiences with cutting meat to resell immediately gave me some skills that were put to good use at the farm. Every few weeks my father-in-law, Neal, rounded up the newborn calves to process them. This involved vaccinating them, putting a tag in their ears for identification, and castrating the baby bulls. Neal would vaccinate them and put the tag the ears, and he taught me to castrate the bull calves while Carl and a hired hand held each the calf. I got pretty good at this job and became part of the processing crew. Even today I use my butchering skills. I can single-handedly dress a deer from start to finish, gutting, skinning, cutting up, and wrapping it up for the freezer or dehydrating homemade venison jerky. I have butchered many fat hogs for our family's use, and in the past, I have been part of the crew along with Carl's parents, butchering fat calves.

However, Carl has always been a little queasy around blood, so he never made it as part of the butchering team.

A few years after we were married, we had a farrowing house, where the sows delivered their litters. We would vaccinate them, dock their tails, trim their sharp little needle teeth so they wouldn't bite their mommas, and castrate the males. Sometimes the sows had complications in labor, and because my hands were small enough to reach in to pull the pigs, I could help in their safe deliveries. The sow was in a pen where she could not turn to attack me, so I was braver than I would have been if the sow were loose. After the piglets were ready to be weaned, we moved them to the nursery, where they received booster shots and any necessary care. Once the pigs grew to about sixty pounds or so, they were transferred to the finishing house, the third location where they remained until they were fat enough for market. On the day of sorting, I became very accurate in eyeballing each hog, knowing if it were heavy enough to go to market. This was valuable because if we sent underweight hogs, they were discounted. We could even get a bonus if the entire load was composed of hogs of approximately the same weight, so my skills helped us gain more profit.

By and by, when the kids got a little older, I learned to drive the tractor. The first time I helped was in the hayfield. The tractors at the time had a clutch that was like driving a stick shift, and I was a little rough on my stops and starts. Because of this, the men learned to hang on tight, but I was cheap help, and they survived.

Neal was the combine man, and one day he said, "I bet you could learn to run this thing, blondie." (That was his favorite nickname for me.) He showed me how to run the combine, while Carl and the hired help hauled the grain to the bin or to the elevator to sell. The combine is more complicated than most of the tractors, so after I ran the combine a few years, the guys would tell me they were sure I could figure out how to run any new tractor we got. As the newer models came out, they had more automatic features, so we did not have to shift through each gear, which was certainly much easier. It was also safer for someone as inexperienced as I was to have more confidence while backing up to connect to any sort of implement. When I backed up using a clutch, it was hard to tell the gear, and it might lunge a little instead of slowly and gently nearing the person standing back there to hook it up. Backing up always made me nervous. I was afraid I might smash my helper, so the automatic tractors were a godsend.

In the beginning, I would rake hay in the fields, but only when the men were really in need. With my sensitive allergies and no cab on the old tractor, I would suffer for days being out in the dusty hayfield. Nowadays most of the tractors have air-conditioned cabs, and I am now the main hay raker. The boys and Carl will switch tractors to give me the cab to keep me healthy when I help. Now each summer, Carl and I make a good hay team. After Carl mows the hay, it lies in the field, letting the sun cure it until it is ready to bale. On baling day, Carl and I are the baling team, with Carl baling behind me while I rake the hay into rows for his baler. When I first came around the farm, hay was baled into small, square bales that were very labor-intensive to produce. Small bales are picked up from the ground in the hayfield by hand and bucked up onto a flat-bed trailer. Another worker is on the trailer to stack the bales securely in a weaving pattern so that they do not fall off. As the stack on the trailer increases, the worker really has to use muscle power to buck the fifty-pound bale higher than his head to stack it. Then the load is taken to the barn. A portable hay elevator with a conveyor belt hauls the bales from the trailer up into the barn, where manpower has to stack the bales once again for storage for the winter. A summer hay crew does not have to spend money on tanning beds or gym membership. They are in the sun all afternoon, and they get an intense workout.

Now our family utilizes newer technology with large round bales weighing a quarter-ton to half-ton each and standing up to six feet tall. Our family uses a wrap on each bale to protect it from the elements because we do not store our large bales inside of buildings. At one time, we stored these big bales inside a pole barn, but then we had a problem. One time some of the bales burst into flames from spontaneous combustion. After that incident, we began to simply trust the wraps to protect the hay from the elements as well as they can until we feed them to the cattle.

Even as recently as the summer of 2018, a couple of bales spontaneously combusted into a smolder. The neighbor saw the smoldering and told us so that we could separate them from the rest of the bales. Once a bale begins to smolder, it will burn, and there is nothing anyone can do to stop it. We have to let it burn out. The big bales are much easier to produce and feed to the cattle than the small bales are, and it is nearly impossible to find a strong group of young men to form a hay crew in the summer. We pay for equipment and supplies with the money that once was a teenager's summer salary. Feeding small bales is a daily chore. If you try to feed more than the animals need for one day, the excess will be tromped on and wasted. We can haul large round bales to the cattle and place them in large metal rings, creating a sort of continual self-feeder. The cattle will reach only their heads into the rings and feed on the hay for three or four days, with the rings protecting the hay quality until it is consumed. These rings have certainly saved cattle farmers money and time.

After more than three decades as a farm wife, I now feel comfortable saying I am part of the crop production team. I have the confidence to operate nearly all of the machinery required for field work, such as drilling beans, plowing, disking, or cultivating ground. I have mowed pastures with a hay mower, and I can also use a large Bush Hog mower to keep the brush down in the pastures. The Bush Hog can mow off corn stalks after the fields are harvested and also keep the roadsides on our property trimmed down. Driving the Bush Hog mower has really gotten my adrenaline pumping a couple of times when the bearings or the clutch in the mower went out. One time I was concentrating on my path in front of me and did not notice anything wrong for a while. Eventually, I glanced back and panicked. I saw flames licking up from the mower and lots of smoke billowing out. The dried debris had caught on fire. I jumped out of the tractor and tried to beat out the fire while texting my family for help from whomever was nearest. Then I called anyone who would answer to help me put the fire out. I could not get the mower disconnected, so if the fire increased, the tractor was going to go too. I was rescued by my family, thankfully, who eventually put out the fire. Fortunately, if the family does not answer, I have our neighbor, Michael McDowell, on speed dial for any emergency backup assistance.

Recently, I have learned a new farm skill. The newly harvested grain is usually hauled by semitrucks to grain elevators for sale or else to the farm to be stored in bins or silos. These big trucks do not usually enter the fields because they would make huge ruts or possibly get stuck. The semis are parked on the road or at the edge of the field where gravel gives them firm bases. A grain cart is a large wagon pulled behind a tractor, and it can go to the combine wherever it is in the field to catch grain directly from the combine. The combine unloads the grain into the grain cart, and the grain cart delivers the load to the semi. Most people, when they first begin to help with the harvest, start by driving a grain cart, which is typically not as complicated as operating a combine. I, on the other hand, skipped this step, instead going straight to operating the combine. During the 2018 harvest, I had my first grain cart experience. Even though this job was supposed to be simple, I still felt a little unsure of myself. Because I had no grain cart experience before this, I was satisfied to have no spills or accidents during my one-day stint, and I was thankful to return once again to the familiarity of my combine cab. My regular job with the harvest team is driving the combine, with my teammate Carl driving the grain cart, and our sons hauling the grain away.

Carl and I are teammates on the hay crew and the harvest team. One other example of teamwork comes when we feed the cattle, which begins in late fall when the pastures become dormant after the first frost and continues through the winter until the pastures green up in the spring. This would be just about the same time as city folks begin mowing their lawns. Once or twice a week I will drive the tractor to load two large bales, one on the front and one on the back. Carl opens and closes the gates and cuts the wrap from each bale. I can then place each bale into a metal ring for the cows to enjoy.

One task I cannot do and never want to learn to do is to back up any vehicle with a trailer or wagon behind it. Driving forward is not the problem; backing up is. I cannot get the trailer pointed in the right direction, no matter how hard I try. In fact, several years ago I was sent on a mission in the truck with a small trailer behind it. My destination was a sale barn in Rushville, about forty-five minutes away, and it was my first time there. My load was a rather ornery bull that we needed to sell. All along, I was hoping to not get stranded or stuck somewhere and be required to back up. When I got to the sale barn, I parked by the gate and walked into the office. I said, "If you want this bull, you're going to have to back the trailer to the barn yourself. I only can do forward." They just laughed and backed it in.

Even today, after more than thirty-five years of experience on the farm, I still find unexpected challenges. My tractor driving skills are respectable but not perfect. I had two memorable incidents as recently as spring and fall of 2018.

In the spring, I was mowing one of the pastures, and I misjudged how wet and soggy one of the lowest areas was. I buried my working office (the tractor and mower) that day and had to walk up the hill to get a signal to call for help. The low, soggy area also had no cell phone signal. Go figure.

Later that same year, I was assigned to drill winter wheat. Farmers often plant a cover crop such as rye, wheat, or barley in the fall to help prevent erosion of the topsoil and to add a little fresh grazing for the local wildlife. We sometimes plant wheat as a cover crop for winter, and then, before it matures, we mow it in early spring for wheat hay. Normally we plant beans after the wheat hay is removed. If we want to put that ground back into corn, we would not harvest the wheat for hay but would spray the wheat to kill it and then plant corn there. Corn needs to be planted earlier than beans, and we would not have time for two different crops in our corn field in one season. Drilling wheat is not a precise skill; the rows do not have to be perfectly straight. When the drill behind the tractor is down, then seed is going into the ground. When the drill is lifted, the seed flow is shut off. At the end of each row, you have to slow down the tractor, pull the switch to lift the drill, and then carefully turn around.

On this particular day in the fall of 2018, I misjudged and turned a little too short. Somehow, the drill became wedged on the back tire, and I was stuck. I just sat there and waited for John to help me on his way back from his bean-hauling trip. He freed the drill from the tractor, and I went back to work. I did not realize I had damaged anything at first. However, something just did not feel right. There was not enough pull, and the sound was different. I looked around and saw the problem. As I was driving the tractor forward, my drill was disconnected and rolling backward down the hill toward the ditch. Carl and the boys have learned to check their phones frequently when I am left out on my own. If anything crazy can possibly happen on my watch, it probably will.

I will never forget one incident in the summer of 2018 that gave us quite a scare as a perfectly peaceful, relaxing Sunday afternoon turn into chaos. Billy, our little indoor dog, was intrigued with something behind my recliner, so I finally peeked around to see what was going on. My heart stopped when I saw a huge black snake, coiled with its head raised, staring straight at Billy. I screamed, "*Snake!*" and took off, with Carl right behind me. I scrambled through the kitchen, shoved open the door to the porch, and kept running.

Behind me, Carl shouted, "There's another one!" as we burst out the outside porch door and stood outside, panting and wide-eyed. Though I have a reasonable fear of snakes, Carl has an extreme phobia of the slithering creatures, so I assumed he was exaggerating when he said there was another one. But no, as we peeked back in on the porch, I saw snake number two wrapped around my shoe rack, staring right back at me. In my crazed attempt to flee, I had nearly knocked into it as I flew by! After standing barefoot on the sidewalk, stewing about how to proceed, we eventually reentered the house and removed those two snakes, with my brave husband overcoming his phobia to lead the attack. The only way they could have entered was through a hole the carpenters left when we had some remodeling done. Vowing to stop the reptile invasion, I boarded that gap up tight, and we have been snake-free ever since. This is a vivid reminder of how our lives on the farm can change from peace to hysteria in just one moment.

Hunting has always been a huge part of life on the Kurfman farm. Before I came onto the scene, Carl was an avid raccoon hunter. In fact, when prices for coon pelts were high, Carl hunted and sold enough skins to pay for a brand-new Ford pickup truck. Deer hunting season has always brought the Sonethongkhams to the farm to hunt for some of Pike County's huge, grain-fed whitetail deer. Over the years, I have helped dress, butcher, and process many, many deer. My boys especially enjoy the deer jerky I make, and deer burger is a delicious ingredient in many dishes such as tacos, chili, and spaghetti.

Some of our greatest hunting adventures come in the spring when the delicious morel mushrooms pop up in the timber areas on the farm. Neal's mushroom hunting skills were uncanny, and he taught our family to look for these delicacies, which are available only a few days each spring. Neal almost always found the most mushrooms, so one mushroom experience stands out in my memory as the one time we beat him. In the spring of 1996, Neal came to the house to take John and Nathan out mushrooming on his four-wheeler. Nolan, who was four years old at the time, was devastated to be left behind, so Carl and I took him on another four-wheeler along a fence row. I grabbed one small plastic grocery bag, assuming we wouldn't find enough mushrooms to even fill this one bag. I spotted one mushroom just on the other side of the fence, and Nolan jumped off the four-wheeler to pick it. However, he could not get over the fence. Carl and I both had to get off and one stand on each side to get him over. I noticed a few more mushrooms along the fence, and Nolan was happy to pick those. Before we climbed back over to get on the four-wheeler, I spotted an old tree stump, and growing around it was the biggest patch of mushrooms I had ever seen! Of course, this was before we carried cell phones to document our success. We filled the plastic bag, and Carl took off his T-shirt and filled it also. We were so proud of this find. When we got home, Grandpa and his crew showed up with their respectable mushroom find for the day. However, the huge batch of mushrooms that Carl, Nolan, and I found around that old tree stump was the most we had ever found without Neal's help, and we finally topped the pro. Our family has been so blessed to have adventures like this that we could never experience if we lived in a city.

We have especially fond memories of our favorite wintertime activity when the boys were small: sledding parties. When we received a nice snowfall, we would gather at the home of Gerald and Mary Emma Kurfman, Carl's aunt and uncle. Gerald and Mary Emma lived on Highway 104 near Fishhook, near the clearing that had formerly been the rest area where Carl and I first met. Their snug brick house sat on a hill that sloped down toward the highway—a perfect hill for sledding. My boys, their cousins, and some friends would meet there when it snowed enough. The kids would slide down the hill on sleds, discs, toboggans, or whatever they brought along and then trudge back up to do it over and over again. Gerald would watch all of the action from the front window. When they were cold and exhausted, they took off their cold, wet coats, coveralls, hats, gloves, scarves, and boots in the garage and then came inside the house for Mary Emma's snickerdoodles and hot cocoa.

One time, Nathan was going so fast that he flew down the hill and did not stop until he had streaked completely across the highway. We are so thankful that no one drove past at that time. After that, the adults set up straw bales to keep them from going onto the highway. As the kids got a little older and a little more confident, they also increased their speed and took a few more risks. One of the older cousins, Devin Kurfman, began pulling the younger kids around with the four-wheeler. They started with sleds, but then began improvising with more adventuresome objects as their sleds, using an old truck hood, an old Big Wheel ride toy with the wheels off, and even the top of an old hog shed the boys tore off. The daredevil sledding kids from that time period are now adults, most of them with kids of their own, but they all still remember snow days as some of the best adventures of their youth. A city kid could never imagine the fun entertainment we country folks could devise!

Summertime brought totally different activities on the farm, such as gardening. Every year we have a garden, and our large garden provides many delicious vegetables for our family. I always enjoy raising tomatoes, onions, cucumbers, peppers, green beans, kale, and so many other goodies. I do not can as many of the goods as my mother-in-law used to do, but I do freeze some of the produce to have for soups, stews, and other meals all winter long. One part of the garden is my dad's area, and he plants some of his favorites, including Asian hot peppers, yard beans, Asian eggplant, and various types of Asian squash. I have also planted many flowers around our farmhouse, and I love to see the hummingbirds and butterflies that the blooms attract.

I have always contributed my time and skills on the farm in various ways, but at times, I brought in some additional income through various resources. Before we had kids, I worked at Micro Force in Pittsfield, gaining programming experience for about a year. Then I took a full-time position with Quintron Corporation in Quincy as an entry-level programmer developing cellular phone software. I was there almost two years before our first son, John Richard, was born. I took maternity leave, and I was having a really hard time going back to work, but I did.

That winter John and I were driving home during freezing rain when I lost control of my car on the curve near Liberty. My car spun around a couple of times, coming to rest still on the road but facing the wrong direction. That incident scared me enough to wonder if I should stay home with our boy. About three months after I returned from maternity leave, Quintron started to lay off several employees, and I was one. I must say I was not very upset. I was really rather happy about not having to leave my baby. When my unemployment ran out, Carl and I decided that I needed to be home with our baby. Then Nathan joined us when John was seventeen months old. With two boys, my life was completely full, and I did not have the energy to worry about a job for a few years.

In 1990, with John and Nathan still at home, before Nolan arrived, I became a Mary Kay cosmetics sales representative. Needing to find some adult time and also wanting some spending money, I plunged into my new role, using sales and marketing skills I learned from my mom when we were still in Laos and Thailand. I earned the title of Queen of Sales in our area one year, and I was on target for directorship more than once. However, I refused to give up more of my family time to become a full-time sales director. My family time, especially my boys' ball game schedules, came first. I rarely missed a game.

Nolan joined us in May 1992, and he and I made a team of two to go after parts or run any errands should our men call on us. For several years, I chose to be a stay-at-home mom, but I could not have done this without Carl and his dedication. He worked longer hours to provide for our family so that I could be home with the kids. I was able to help on the farm at times, and we rarely required babysitters. When the boys got a little older, Grandpa Neal might take one or two with him for some quality time. He enjoyed this, and so did they. But overall, my priority was watching my boys and keeping them safe. The farm is a wonderful place to raise children, but many dangers lurk in various places, so I wanted to protect them as best I could. I was blessed to be at home for the first few years of our children's lives. By the time I was ready to find work outside the home, the older boys were in middle school and in sports. We were very fortunate to have my in-laws living only a block from the school. The boys could go there for a snack or to wait before or after practice. Grandma Margaret Jo would watch Nolan for me until I could get home from work to pick him up. What a blessing this was! I probably would not have gone to work if she were not there for the boys each day.

When Nolan started kindergarten, I decided it was time to work outside the home again, and the first job I took was at the USDA office in Pittsfield, Illinois. I helped with the Loan Deficiency Payment program, helping enter the information to help farmers get extra payment from USDA to supplement the low market prices. USDA only had funding to hire me part time, but I worked two years there in this part-time position. Then I decided to seek full-time employment so that our family could benefit from health insurance, and I was hired at Burrus Seed in Arenzville, Illinois, where I remained for six years.

However, when my sister Nang died, leaving her three children aged eight, six, and two years old, we knew we needed to do whatever we could to help them. This is when we moved away from the farm to reside in Quincy, where Nang's husband and children had moved. The daily drive to Arenzville and back was too far. Also, by this time, Neal had passed, and Margaret Jo's health was slipping, so she came to live with us in Quincy. My parents were beginning to require some additional help as well, so I wanted to available to devote time to care for the young and the old. Full-time work was not an option, but I took a part-time job at my youngest brother Noi's Country Financial Insurance office in Quincy. I was able to make some spending money and still have time for the kids and parents.

Mom's health declined over time to the point she was admitted to a nursing home, and this devastated my family and me. Our Asian tradition was to take care of our parents, so we fulfilled this duty even though she was in a facility. One of us had to stay with Mom at all times there in Sunset Home, a wonderful nursing home in Quincy. My dad, Ott, Tay, Tow, and Noi all lived in Quincy, so they took turns staying with Mom at night. I sat with Mom during the day to comfort her, and though she was admitted for comfort care, which usually signaled she was declining, Mom continued to grow stronger rather than decline. I decided to seek employment there at Sunset so I could be near Mom yet still be able to work. I took an accounts payable position and stayed there a year after Mom passed. I was thankful to be able to give my service to a wonderful nursing home that was so good to my mom.

Volunteering to help the community has always been important to me. I served as an election judge for a few years in our tiny Fishhook voting poll site until we moved to Quincy. Now that we are back in the community, I feel it is about time for me to volunteer to serve again as an election judge because our small community does not have many available volunteers. The compensation is quite small in our little township, so the service is a donation of time rather than an actual paid position. Another opportunity to serve came to me when I was asked to serve on the Pike County Farm Service Agency in Pittsfield. My former boss from my part-time job at the USDA office asked me to consider serving, and I was flattered. I must have shown some promise if my former boss asked me to serve as one of his bosses. I accepted the offer, and I am looking forward to doing whatever I can to better the agriculture in our area—an important cause in my heart.

As a young girl growing up in Laos, and even as my family crossed the ocean to arrive in America, I could never have anticipated what my future held. However, I have loved my farm life, even with the challenges that come with it. I know my sons have benefitted by growing up working and playing on our family farm. We have been blessed indeed.

chapter 16

My Early Faith

As I look back on my childhood, the earliest memory I have of stating my faith was at school filling out a form that asked my religion. I put Buddhism because that was the only religion I had ever been exposed to.

Our family had few books, but one book I do remember was about Siddhartha Gautama, the Buddha. I looked at the pictures for many years, but as I became old enough to read, I read it from cover to cover. I wanted to know what it was about. It explained who he was and where he came from. He was born in wealth and luxury in Lumbini (now located in Nepal), and when he eventually left his royal enclosure, he saw poverty for the first time. He became a monk and adopted a life of poverty for a while. Neither the wealthy life nor the poverty-filled life satisfied him. He meditated and studied for six years before finding the middle path and enlightenment. He taught his beliefs as principles of Buddhism (dhamma, or truth) for approximately forty-five years until his death at age eighty. Today, there are approximately 376 million followers worldwide, as compared to approximately 1.2 billion Christians.

My parents practiced Buddhism, which, of course, influenced me. I certainly looked forward to all the festivals and fun activities at the temple. As young people, we enjoyed the social aspects of these events. We were too busy with our schooling, helping at home, and, in our case, surviving the war around us, to worry much about our faith and what it meant.

Our language had words for heaven (ສະຫວັນ) and hell (ນະຣົກ). In the temple, hell was depicted with gruesome murals that covered the entire wall. As a little girl, I remember seeing a man with a big, long spear pushing someone's head into a huge vat of something boiling, with flames under the vat. It was a vivid image of torture and a place we needed to fear. Mom would often repeat what her Grandma Vadd (the same grandma who had taught her as a child to pray to a higher power) had told her about such a horrible place. Great-Grandma Vadd believed that if we did not "do good," we might end up in the "bad place." No one wanted to go there, and we were trained to be generous with what we had as a way to avoid the bad place. Our word for how we were to act was *chai boun* (ໃຈບຸນ), which means having a generous heart for others. We were to share what we owned and help others any way we could, especially our parents.

It was considered a disgrace if your parents struggled and you did nothing to help them. Not caring for your parents was believed to be one of the worst sins (ບາບ) you could commit and severe enough to land you in hell. We were trained to believe that only bad people went to hell, and I made certain that I had done enough good works to stay out of there.

On the other hand, if you were referred to as a chai boun person, this was the highest level of respect. There was no clear and certain instruction about how to go to heaven. No one knew much more than doing enough good works would help you stock up *dai boun* (ໄດ້ບຸນ), which was similar to credit in an account that you could hope would keep you out of the bad place when you take your last breath. Buddhists believe that we all have more than one soul; in fact, nearly every part of your body has a separate soul. Also, they believe in reincarnation. If a person was decent enough here on earth, he would hope that was enough to keep him out of hell. No one knew how much he had to do to get to heaven, but with reincarnation each person could hope to get another chance to try again. This could go on over and over without limit.

Even reaching heaven or hell was not necessarily complete or final. With each person possessing many souls, perhaps some of your souls made it to heaven, and some did not. That is why some souls needed more chances to try again, hoping for better results with each life, hopefully landing more souls in heaven the next time. No one would dare utter the thought that even one soul of a deceased person might have ended up in hell. It would be so disrespectful of the memory of the deceased and his or her family. I never heard anyone speak unkindly about someone's memory.

Buddhists believed in spirits and were always a little leery. This apprehension really ramped up to high alert in certain situations, especially if a person died unexpectedly. We did not have medical knowledge to understand heart attacks or strokes; an unexpected death was often interpreted as the person was not ready to go. The lost spirit would linger to haunt those left behind. During the wake at the house, people were very apprehensive that the spirit of the deceased might be lurking there, ready to jump out at them. They listened for every sound or movement and did not go into a dark room or outside alone. As the wake ended, a monk usually arrived to drive the bad spirit out of the house. The family would put a string all the way around the house, and the monk would bless it. This would prevent the bad spirit from getting back in the house. For some reason, the thoughts of these spirits never really spooked me. I used to enjoy pranking people, jumping out at them in the dark just to hear them scream.

Reincarnation was drilled into us through various tales handed down to us. For example, sometimes I heard legends of how a certain young child might remember his or her previous life in detail. Of course, because only that person could have such knowledge, no one could check for facts. I never witnessed firsthand anyone who remembered more than his current life on earth. Occasionally, when a family had a newborn, an acquaintance of the family (or perhaps even the new parent) might have some sort of dream that a deceased relative was coming to move in with them. This would be taken as a sign that the new baby was the reincarnation of the dead relative. No one could prove them wrong, so the belief often flourished. Another belief I remember hearing was that if a woman lived a very good life here on earth, showing much chai boun, then even if she didn't quite make it to heaven, she might at least be able to return as a male. This would be considered a higher position than her life as a lowly woman.

An example of the influence of reincarnation in our family concerned the seventh child, my brother Tow. When he was a baby, he was a content, wonderful baby all day. However, as soon as the sun set, he began to cry, and he would cry all night. We could not console him until daylight appeared. Mom and two of our cousins who lived with us at the time took shifts walking with him all night. (As mentioned earlier, during our flight from Khongsedone, Tow was the crying baby who drew the attention of the Issara soldier who peered into the window while we were supposed to be hiding out in Napong.) An elderly neighbor lady in Saphai heard Tow crying all night for several nights. She finally spoke to my mom and told her that Tow might be trying to give Mom a message about something. This lady knew of a medium who might be able to help Mom figure out what Tow was trying to say. Mom took her up on the offer. The medium told Mom that Tow was her Grandma Vadd reincarnated. Apparently, my mom needed to acknowledge and welcome her. The medium helped my mom plan the ritual to acknowledge and welcome her deceased grandmother. After the ritual Mom performed, within a fairly reasonable time, Tow quit crying. Of course, to Mom, this was concrete evidence to seal her belief that Tow was, in fact, her reincarnated Grandma Vadd, who must have certainly performed many good deeds in her previous life as a woman; here she was in a baby boy's form. I look back now, and I think that possibly Tow had colic and by this time, he may have outgrown it. No matter what I believe or what really happened, my mom believing it and retelling it to others in the family kept the belief in reincarnation alive.

The strong need to do good deeds for your family members does not stop when your loved ones pass. They believe their deceased family still have needs, such as food and shelter. For example, Buddhists continue sacrificing food to their deceased loved ones by taking a portion of their food to the temple as an offering to the deceased. Whenever you make a dish that you know your loved one really enjoyed, you could take some to the temple as a sacrifice. Around lunchtime, several people might bring food in memory of their loved ones, and the monks bless the food and then consume some of it. After they are finished eating, the monks chant prayers for the deceased loved ones to receive the offerings of that day. They will then tell you that it is time for ຫຍາດ ຯ or *yardnom* (pouring water during prayer). After a bit, the monk tells all the people there that it is time to call to the spirits of their loved ones. While the monks are chanting, you can pray to your dead relative, calling him or her by name to come and receive the food you sacrifice as you do yardnom, or pour water to honor the deceased. Sacrificing to your deceased loved ones is one example of a good deed to help you work your way to becoming a chai boun person. This honors the deceased and also provides an additional good deed of feeding the monks in the temple. Anyone could do this daily if desired, so no matter your finances, you were able to participate in a good work like this. Sacrificing food to loved ones who had passed was a small-scale good deed.

Buddhists could also perform good deeds to honor deceased loved ones on a larger scale. They called these deeds ເຮັ ⌣ ຄບຸ,ນ, or *hed boun* (a grand tribute to the deceased). If someone's finances allowed this, a person could plan and pay for a huge celebration to honor one or more of his or her deceased loved ones. The host would absorb all the expense for food, alcohol, and entertainment, which usually meant live music performances. This festival might cost as much as a wedding. The monk attended and called the loved one(s) by name, honoring the deceased. A money tree was filled with donations from the host and guests and given to the monk. All these donations of money, food, and well-wishes were considered to be given to the deceased. This was a hed boun, a high honor tribute to the loved one, not to mention an extreme expense for the host.

Most chai boun people who could afford it would be happy to carry out this hed boun, intending to uplift and provide more good deeds for their loved ones who have passed, hopefully helping provide for them in their afterlife. Here in America, wealthy people might donate a large sum of money in memory of their loved one, hoping to see their loved one's name on a building or facility as a lasting tribute to that special person, so the concept is not entirely foreign to our culture. Buddhists may repeat their hed boun more than once for a person, or perhaps a different host from a different location altogether might offer a separate hed boun for the same deceased person.

Sometimes some chai boun people might hold a hed boun at

the temple to raise money for the work there. This is one way a chai boun person could accumulate more dai boun in their account, so to speak. When it is held at the temple for a fundraiser, it is more like a festival or fair atmosphere. The temple might need remodeling, or perhaps even a completely new building might be required. Money is needed for cleaning, fencing, or any other work to be done there. This is considered a great way to contribute and earn more dai boun. Buddhism does not have a required amount for people to offer. People just give generously as they can whenever they see a need.

Reflecting on my childhood and my experience with Buddhism, I realize I did not have any connection at all with Siddhartha Gautama, Buddhism's founder. As a matter of fact, I could not even say his name until I researched for this writing. I would have been considered to have had an adequate education by my people's standard, yet my general education did not include studying the theology of Buddhism. I believe that most people I knew from my childhood who followed the philosophy of Buddhism did not know the name of Siddhartha Gautama, just like me. We never heard his name mentioned at any temple services. Instead, we were following a how-to-live manual that guided our interactions with others, not really honoring or worshipping the founder of Buddhism.

Traveling to America did not require us to drastically change how we lived and how we interacted with others. We had no reason to change. People around us in our new environment were not disturbed or offended by us because we were respectful, kind, and generous, taking care of one another's needs. We did not come here to find a new way of life; we came here to find a safer environment to live the life we already knew. We were looking for a way to stay together without interference from those in power.

We were looking for a way to avoid dangerous conflicts that seemed to find us wherever we were in Laos.

What I noticed when I observed those who followed the Buddhist philosophy was that they had freedom to add or subtract any rituals as they felt appropriate. I can remember how Buddhists who lived north of us in Laos observed a one-hundred-day celebration when they lost loved ones, but my area had never heard of this celebration. This was a man-made ritual that you could choose to observe or not. Also, followers of Buddhism were not required to follow only Buddhism; they could practice other philosophies. For example, my mother's family, because of their Chinese heritage, practiced food sacrifices to their ancestors. This differed from the Buddhists' sacrifices at the temple for the monks to consume; when Mom's family sacrificed to their ancestors, they consumed the food themselves after the ritual ended. These food sacrifices would be offered on several holidays, such as the anniversary of the loved one's death, Chinese New Year, and a special Memorial Day set aside to take food to the cemetery to sacrifice at the loved ones' graves. This is an example of how followers of Buddhism were free to practice other beliefs as long as they did not do harm to others or result in any laws broken.

Someone might think that an Asian family coming to America might resist attending church here. However, we tried very hard to be respectful to our sponsors. We would never tell them no when they wanted us to attend church. We owed them a huge favor for bringing us here, and we would not want to offend them in any way. We assumed everyone here in America was Christian, and we wanted to know what we needed to do to get along in our new homeland. Thankfully, our Buddhist beliefs did not restrict us from other practices or philosophies, so our family was more receptive to new ideas. We were actually eager to learn more from these generous people who had been so kind to us in our struggles.

We did not have their language to comprehend their words, but we could feel their genuine love, and this drew us to them. My head and my eyes showed me earthly things I had received from our sponsors, but my heart could truly feel their genuine love for Jesus, who was their Lord. I could not understand their intentions at that time; I just felt their love. I had my first taste of Jesus's love through this group of Christians. This love planted a seed in me—a gift that I did not seek and one that I did not even know existed—but this seed of love grew in my heart and led me to a decision that definitely shaped my life here on earth as well as for eternity.

chapter 17

A Double Blessing

No one could deny that coming to America was a blessing for our family. When we made the decision to come here, we had simply hoped for the basics—food and shelter—and for all of us to be together, safe from dangerous war zones. Thanks to our sponsors, we had all this provided and so much more. The transition to living in America was difficult. My parents had such passion for us to better ourselves here, and my dad especially focused on education. He knew education was the way out of poverty. In fact, Dad valued schooling so much that when each of us considered marriage, one of the most important requests he had was that our future spouses would be willing to better themselves through education. Anyone who came around our house showing interest in one of us had better show an interest in education as well; otherwise, Dad would not be likely to give his blessing.

When Carl and I were married, Dad was hesitant to give his blessing on our marriage until Carl promised to support me in my final year of schooling to finish my degree. It took lots of hard work to earn a living and to get our education, and our language barrier made everything even more difficult. The caring Christian families from the First Presbyterian Church in Quincy helped make this transition easier, mentoring all of us, taking us various places to provide many enriching experiences, and providing information about how to not just get by in America but how to thrive. I am so thankful for the wonderful new life we gained here.

Blessings can be funny things; sometimes you may receive one even when you are not expecting it. Besides finding all my physical needs met, another even greater blessing that I received here in America was finding the way to have eternal life with Jesus. I was not even looking for this when I came here, but several people cared enough for me to plant seeds of faith, and God took care of the rest.

It took time for me to me to accept Jesus as my Savior. In college, I studied computer programming, which is based on using logic, looking at data, analyzing problems, and finding solutions. My computer programming brain wants to see proof of why something does or does not work. A computer programmer repeatedly asks, "What if?" in the job. If the first "What if?" doesn't work, he goes back and looks for something else and finds another way to see the problem. All the data should provide proof for what works. When I heard that accepting Jesus as my Savior was the way to spend eternity in heaven, my fact-based brain had trouble letting go and allowing my heart to simply believe.

It took me a while to allow my faith to grow. It is sometimes hard to explain faith, but I think of it as believing from your heart rather than seeing proof with your eyes. Some of the most important things in life are felt with your heart, not your eyes. For example, when you fall in love with someone, you begin to feel who that person is, not always counting on physical sight. In fact, you begin to overlook small flaws, only feeling love from your heart. You will close your eyes when you kiss, not needing to see the face, but just to feel the love. We do this with our children as well. Your child may do or say things that disappoint you, but because your heart controls your feelings, you still love that child, not allowing the behaviors seen with the eye to destroy that love. When a person prays, he often closes his eyes, knowing that he does not need to see the One receiving the prayers. Whether adoring your sweetheart, loving a child, or praying, you no longer need to use your eyes—your heart leads you. From that moment on, you walk by faith, not by sight.

Our family attended church at First Presbyterian when we moved to Quincy. At first, we were picked up every week, and later, when Dad got his car, he drove us there. So we all heard Bible messages throughout the first few years we were here. However, as I grew older and attended college, I began working Sunday mornings at the college cafeteria, so I was no longer attending with my family.

First Presbyterian Church succeeded in planting solid seeds of faith, but my soil was pretty rough. The seeds would not grow until Carl came along. When I started dating Carl, he invited me to attend Fishhook United Brethren Church. The minister, Clifford Phillips, lived in Quincy, so he and his wife, Opal, offered to give me a ride each Sunday morning. Even though I hated missing out on money from my cafeteria job, I quit it and agreed to come with Clifford and Opal. The drive from Quincy to Fishhook was about forty minutes, and Clifford would visit with me on the way. Of course, he had to keep the conversation simple because I still struggled with English.

I was taking a religion course in college, and Clifford would ask about that. I would share what I had learned. Clifford asked me what I thought of other religions. Before my religion class, I had no concept of different faiths. Buddhism does not tell you to question other faiths or to hate other believers. I was looking more at the rituals they performed. For example, I remember one week we had studied about how some Native Americans used above=ground burial platforms. Clifford asked me what I thought about this. I told him I had no problem with any religion as long as we could coexist peacefully instead of going to war against one another.

At this point, we were driving through the small town of Liberty, and Clifford had to slow down. I remember this moment very clearly. Clifford said, "Let me tell you a little bit about Christianity." I had learned a few things about Christianity from our attendance at First Presbyterian Church. I knew that December 25 was a celebration of Jesus's birth, and we all loved the food and gifts. On Easter I heard the message about Jesus's death and resurrection. I was looking at these celebrations as rituals, similar to the festivals I had enjoyed in my homeland.

Clifford explained to me that Jesus was the only One who died and rose again. All other religions were founded by men who were still in the grave. When Clifford said this, something changed in me, and I began to feel a warm glow. The salvation seed began to take root in my heart that day. Perhaps that was the proof my logical mind had needed.

Sometimes you just know some things. You ponder them and put them in your heart, but you don't totally understand them. That is how I was with accepting Jesus. I had to be certain it was better than what I already had, more promising, just like leaving my homeland. In my youth, I had heard people who left Laos had better lives, and I wanted this for myself and my family. I was willing to take the chance of escaping with all the risks involved, leaving my home, and learning a new language and culture for this opportunity. When I heard the salvation message, I kept looking at the promise of eternal life with Jesus, and it began to be something I knew I wanted, a blessed hope.

Naturally, my computer-programming brain battled against

my faith for a while. I had to look at what I had always believed as opposed to believing in Jesus and ask the what-ifs that I had.

- ✦ What if Christians were right about only having one soul instead of several?
- ✦ What if Christians were right about only having one life, one chance to decide where to spend eternity instead of numerous chances to be reincarnated and try again?
- ✦ What if salvation really is a gift and there is no way to earn it with good works?
- ✦ And a huge one for me: What if I would be separated forever from my family by choosing to accept Jesus?

I did not decide right away. I waited for a while, taking time to compare my previous belief with the Christian faith, asking if my way was better. Deep down, I knew it was not better; I really did not have a way to be certain to go to heaven. With time, my heart and my brain finally lined up, and after reflecting on all my what-ifs, I chose to accept Jesus as my Savior, even though I knew I could possibly be outcast from my own family and people I knew and loved.

My belief grew. One day during the altar call, the minister asked for anyone who had not accepted Christ to repeat after him, either aloud or silently, "I believe Jesus is the Son of the living God." I repeated this silently. I do not remember who the minister was or when this happened, but I remember repeating this and knowing I had accepted Jesus as my Savior. By this time, we had John, and I had heard about how babies and small children would be in Heaven if they died young; they were too young to choose where to go. I remember I wanted to be sure to go where my husband and children would go for eternity.

My faith was real, and it continued to grow from the time Clifford told me what it meant to be a Christian, but my heart was not yet burdened to tell anyone else about my decision, and I had not yet professed my faith publicly. Eventually, after Nathan was born, I was ready to tell others. I wanted to be baptized to make a public profession of my faith, and Rev. Mark Dickerson performed my baptism in the Baptist Church in Griggsville because our little Fishhook church did not have a baptistry. Mom and Dad attended, which meant a lot to me. This is when I began to let others know where I would be spending eternity. I knew I was taking a chance that I might be separated from my family, but I prayed that instead, I would be the person who would lead my loved ones to heaven so we can be together after we leave this earth.

What holds you back? What are your what-ifs keeping you from wanting a relationship with Jesus? Sometimes people show an interest in Jesus, but think, *Not now. Maybe I will decide later.*

I say to these people, "Do not linger. You are not sure of the next day." I had time to reason it all out, but some people do not.

I think about how hard it was to navigate our way out of Laos, out of Thailand, and into our home in America. It would have been so much better if we had a navigation system to show us each step of the way. I believe I now have my life's GPS turned on, and the destination is set to go straight to heaven. This GPS is available to anyone, and I invite you to accept this free gift today.

My family and I sought a better life in America, and I am so thankful that I received this blessing. However, I could not have known that an even greater blessing waited for me here—the chance to accept Jesus and eternal life in heaven. I thank God for my double blessing.

chapter 18

A Forwarding Address

I have a saying about life here on earth. "No one makes it out alive." I do not mean to be disrespectful; this is how I feel when I consider how we leave our earthly bodies. But when we leave this life as we know it, where will we go? Is there a way to know for sure how to find loved ones after they pass from this earth? As a Christian, I view earth as my current address, but heaven is my forwarding address. If you want to find me after I am gone, that is where you need to go.

We all know our birth date but, unfortunately, not our death date. Nobody knows how many days we have left here on earth. For example, my sister Nang was taken without warning at age thirty-eight while her husband and children prepared her breakfast. She had been feeling a little ill and was resting at home. She said she was feeling hungry and requested breakfast. When they brought it up, she did not respond; she had already passed.

I know my sister had heard about Jesus from various encounters. Mom and Dad dutifully took us to First Presbyterian Church each Sunday while we were still living at home. I was actually the first one to stray away from attending every week when I got a job, and each of my siblings followed my steps, one by one, as obligations and schedules got in the way. But still, Nang had attended many services, youth group activities, and Sunday school classes where the Gospel would have been shared. Later on, one summer, when Nang was in college, she traveled with Sister Ann, a nun from Quincy University, on a missionary trip. I assume she helped tell others about Jesus then. Another comfort I have is that I know she took her children to vacation Bible school in Rochester, Minnesota, where they lived. Even though she had never told me that the kids had attended VBS, one summer when I was visiting Nang, I helped her clean her car and found several Bible school papers that her kids had left behind. Also, our son John lived for a time with Nang, and she occasionally attended church with him. One more connection with Christianity was that Sister Ann, originally from Quincy, moved to Rochester and was there when Nang was, and they kept in touch.

After Nang's death, I know that Lith, her husband, struggled with his grief. However, I believe he is a Christian, and he has the blessed hope to be reunited with Nang one day in heaven. Lith was devoted to following the philosophy of Siddhartha Gautama, the Buddha, while still in Laos. I knew he, as many other young Lao men, had been a monk at one time, studying at the temple, dedicated to worship and learning more of Buddhist philosophy. Just a short while ago, I learned that as a child, he had attended a private school run by Christian nuns in Laos. For some time, I was aware that Lith had been reading the Bible, including Nang's Bible with her notes in it. However, the most wonderful indicator of Lith's new faith in Jesus Christ was when he told me how thankful he was that he found the true God. If he had stayed in Laos, he would still believe in man. What a powerful testimony of a believer in Jesus!

None of us could have predicted Nang's swift passing from this earth, but my mother, on the other hand, had years of warning that her time was near. First, she developed high blood pressure and then diabetes, taking shots for many years. At age fifty-six, she suffered her first heart attack. That was in 1996. Her health declined from that point on due to a combination of problems. She suffered from rheumatoid arthritis and lupus and had to take a handful of pills daily for these problems. A couple of years after these health problems began, Nang brought her to Mayo Clinic, where Nang worked as a computer programmer for the information system there. There, the medical staff helped Mom feel better and improve for a short time.

However, after Nang died in February 2006, it seems that Mom's health declined even more quickly. The stress and grief multiplied Mom's physical pain. Her Buddhist upbringing and traditions did not provide any hope for her or anyone else to see loved ones again after they died. Mom had no hope to ever see Nang again; it was a complete, permanent, painful loss for her. I saw how devastated Mom was, and I also saw how fearful she was about her own death. I was suffering to watch her in this agony. I too was suffering from losing Nang, but I had a hope that one day I would see Nang again in heaven. I was reassured that she knew who Jesus was based on her mission work, vacation Bible school, and church attendance. I could dare to hope that she had a personal relationship with Jesus, accepting Him as her Savior, and this helped me cope with the loss of my dear sister.

The summer of 2006 brought Nang's husband and children to Quincy to live closer to family as they coped with losing Nang. After twenty-four years on the farm, Carl and I decided to move to Quincy to help with Nang's children. At this point, Mom's health was deteriorating so much that our move there was a blessing for her as well. Our youngest, Nolan, was a freshman in high school, so he completed his schooling at Quincy High School while we tended to family and helped as we could.

In winter of 2009, a routine checkup with Mom's heart

specialist indicated she had some blockage in her arteries and suggested that she needed an outpatient catheterization to put in stents. This was supposed to be a simple, safe procedure. However, after about a week, she began to have some side effects from this procedure. She had severe pain in her right toe and foot, and we took her to the emergency room. They admitted her to administer strong pain medications such as morphine to help control the pain. She received so much pain medication that she was basically in a sedated state for several days. At that time, Sing and I had hospital duty, while the rest of the brothers were on their annual ski trip to Colorado. Mom was in so much pain that she wanted someone to massage her feet to help ease the pain a bit. This was when we noticed that her middle toe on her right foot had a black spot, like deep bruising, but we did not realize this spot was the start of a grueling decline for mom's foot. The doctors and nurses did not seem overly concerned about it because they sent her home with lots of pain medicines.

After she had been home for a few days, we noticed her toe's black spots were worsening, spreading more and drying up, looking a little like jerky. We were not doctors, but in our hearts, we knew something was not right. We feared this might be a sign that the flesh was dying. At an appointment for a checkup with her regular doctor, our suspicion was confirmed. Her toes were dying. The doctor said the only way to get rid of the pain was to amputate her right foot. For her amputation to heal, she needed good circulation, and the lower right leg's circulation would not supply enough blood flow to heal the wound. They would have to amputate below the knee. By this time, her left foot was having some issues as well. During the presurgery circulation test, the left foot had no blood flow to the toes. However, she had better circulation clear down through her left ankle, so the doctor recommended to amputate only her toes on the left while she was undergoing the right leg amputation below the knee, saving her from having to come back for a second procedure.

After her surgery, Mom struggled to recover. Another test showed that she needed another stent in her artery, but Mom refused. She was aware that the earlier procedure most likely caused her clots from the plaque to be loosened and caused the toes to die. She signed a do-not-resuscitate form. She would not allow more procedures to prolong her life, such as another heart catheterization. Mom was giving up fighting to stay here on earth. She had suffered enough. The medical staff were adamant that if she did not have the heart procedure right then, she would have a major heart attack, and she would be gone—possibly that night. We family members were not given much hope for her survival. We gathered around her to say goodbye. Her extended family began to fly in from all over, including Canada and France, hoping to get there in time to say goodbye and to be there for the funeral. We were trying to prepare to begin our lives without her.

That night came and passed, yet Mom remained with us. Her pain was from her amputation wound rather than the excruciating toe pain she had been suffering before. Each day, the doctors remained confident she would soon die. After lingering for a few days like this, the doctor recommended for Mom to go on Hospice and transfer to a nursing home for her final days. She was placed on comfort care there.

After about a week there, Mom showed some signs that she was getting stronger rather than weakening. The staff asked if we minded if they worked her arms and legs to keep her strength up, and we agreed, if she wasn't hurt by it. Her leg and amputation site were not the only problem spots. Mom began to complain about pain in various places, such as her belly. Soon after she complained of pain in a certain spot, a dark area would appear there, and the flesh would sink in like a tiny bowl. These were apparently more areas where pieces of plaque lodged and blocked her circulation. She had multiple wounds of various sizes and depths on her body. Even though Mom had so much suffering to deal with, she did have a blessing with these wounds. None developed on her back, so she was able to lie in bed without putting pressure on these sore areas. Her time in the nursing home was for her to die, not to recover, so the nurses' orders were that they simply try to comfort her the best they could.

After a couple of months, she stopped developing new wounds. The nurse who dressed her amputation wound noticed that the area there showed some slight improvement, as if she might have a chance to heal with proper care. By this time, no one was mentioning Hospice anymore, and instead, the medical staff wanted to see if she might heal even more successfully with the proper care. They sent her to a wound clinic to get her wounds trimmed and cleaned, and she was placed in a hyperbaric chamber, which had a high concentration of oxygen to promote healing. We kept up this regimen for six months, and her wounds were healing. Mom was not ready to leave this earth quite yet.

Mom had not walked since her amputation; she had been bedridden. With the wounds healing so nicely, the nursing home suggested that Mom might be able to get a prosthetic right leg and a specially designed shoe for her left foot and possibly walk again. This was not a quick fix; she was in therapy for over a year before she could take a step. But she did it! She learned to walk with a walker, and she was able to come home.

Even though Mom was home, she was dependent on help for everything from walking to personal care. She did not have pain, but she knew she would never be totally independent, and this was depressing to a woman who was such a hard worker, always taking care of others. She was happy to be home but also struggling minute to minute with fears and anxiety.

One day I came to visit her, and she was discussing her discontent. I began a discussion with her. Mom's belief was that she would come back, reincarnated in another form. I asked Mom if she loved everything about this life on earth so much that she would want to come back and repeat it. She thought for a moment and said, "Not really."

This opened a door for me to share where I would be going. I told her that I would be with Jesus after I leave this earth. The chance that she and I would ever see each other again was almost impossible. I would not return to this earth; I would be in heaven. Lots of people she knew would be there. I listed some that I knew believed in Jesus, such as my in-laws, Mrs. Oakley, and Mr. and Mrs. Turner. Of course, I hope that Nang is there, waiting for me as well. I told my mom that it was very important for her to tell me where she wanted to be after she left this earth.

Little by little, I knew that Mom was thinking over what I had said. She began to ask more questions, and I would answer them as best I could. It was difficult to translate into Lao so that she would understand and not lose the meaning. One day while we were in the doctor's waiting room for an appointment, we again struck up a conversation. She asked how to know for sure she could go to heaven. I told her it's by faith. If you believe that Jesus is the Son of God and you ask Him to come into your heart to be your Lord, you will go to heaven. I told her that out of all the different leaders of different beliefs in the world, Jesus is the only one who came to earth, died, and rose to go to heaven. This separates Him from human leaders and prophets. I said if she wanted to join Jesus's family, I would lead her, and she could repeat after me. She said she wanted this. I led her through a statement of faith, and she willingly repeated after me. I asked her if she wanted to be baptized by Kevin McGinnis, a family friend from First Presbyterian Church who was an associate pastor at the time. She said yes, and as soon as we left the doctor's office, we went straight to the church where she was baptized. Her public profession of faith was witnessed by Kevin and me, and it was a beautiful moment. After becoming so dependent on others for her every need, she now had a chance to take charge of her own journey in her life by accepting the free offer of eternity in heaven with Jesus.

After Mom was home about a year, she had a major stroke and never regained consciousness. She died on January 10, 2012. I suspect that more plaque came loose and lodged in her brain, finally taking her from this earth and all her physical suffering.

Mom's salvation was a real blessing to me, but the only regret I have is that she did not have time to mature in her belief enough to share about Jesus with her loved ones before she passed. Dad, especially, misses Mom and longs to see her again. In fact, he still sets out a cup of coffee each morning, a sort of food sacrifice that helps him feel closer to her. Dad's father, Grandpa Liam, served as an elder in the Buddhist Temple, coordinating the festivals and overseeing building maintenance and provision for the monks. So Dad's Buddhist upbringing was engrained in him from a young child, and this training did not offer Dad a clear and direct path to reunite with Mom in eternity, believing in reincarnation rather than an eternal life in heaven. Ever since Mom passed, Dad has been yearning for her, clearly thinking of her each morning when he sets out her coffee. Even though I knew the only way Dad will see Mom eternally is to accept Jesus as his Savior, his deep Buddhist beliefs would not allow him to hear the Good News. Over and over, I shared that Jesus is the only way to heaven. Time and time again, Dad would shut off my attempts to explain who Jesus is, telling me he did not care where he was going. He would go where his ancestors were, back to the earth to be reincarnated again. This was a heavy burden for me, and my prayers intensified.

Technology is a miracle in some ways. I have used a Bible app for years on my cell phone, but in January 2019, I was clicking around on the app when I discovered that the Bible was available in more than 1,200 languages. And yes … Laotian was a choice! Would Dad be interested in this? A few days later, I was visiting Dad, and I said, "Look what I found!" I began reading Genesis 1 in Lao, struggling a little from my lack of practice. Dad went to get his glasses and followed along to help me sound it out.

When we finished the first chapter, we talked about it, and Dad wanted to know more. We continued for a couple more chapters, but then I had to leave. This was the first time Dad had shown interest in learning about the Bible, and I was thrilled! He had no problem believing that God created the heavens and earth and all creatures, including the first man and woman. The next couple of visits, I would review what we had read and then we would continue reading. Dad showed a great interest in the description of Noah's Ark, trying to visualize it. When we figured the Ark was 133 meters long, Dad commented that it was longer than a soccer field. He was very impressed.

We invited him to join us on our next trip to visit his grandson Nathan in Lexington, Kentucky, near the Ark Encounter. Carl and I took him and his friend Souvanny (we call her Grandma 2) to see the replica of the ark, built to the exact dimensions from the Bible. During the tour, Grandma 2 used a machine to make an ark penny as a souvenir. Dad said, "I might want to make that into a necklace charm since I quit wearing my Buddhist charm due to my new belief."

My heart leaped with joy to think that the seed of salvation was taking root in Dad's heart. Since that day, Dad has read the Gospels in the New Testament. He dug out an old Lao Bible from the basement. Someone had given him this Bible when we first came to Quincy nearly forty years ago. The print was tiny and contained only the New Testament, but he was hungry to read more and learn more. Carl and I ordered a new larger print complete version in Laotian. When I realized Dad was reading the Gospels, I asked him who he thinks Jesus is. He said with confidence that he knows who Jesus is; He is the Son of God, not Joseph's son. All the prayers for Dad's salvation, my prayers as well as the prayers of so many other believers, are softening his heart to recognize the Good News. I now can begin to hope that my dad will meet Mom again when his days on earth are expired.

Though we left Laos as a family of ten, Mom and Dad's family has continued to grow here in America. Mom, unfortunately, did not have the opportunity to meet any of her great-grandchildren before she passed.

I am the eldest, or number one child. Carl and I were blessed with three sons: John Richard in 1985, Nathan Carl in 1987, and Nolan Song in 1992. Nathan married Nina Johnson, and they had Penelope (Penny) Marie in 2017. (Yes, we finally had a little baby girl in the family!) They also had Dominic (Dom) Nathan in 2019. Nolan married Karoline (Karli) Harvey, and they had Neal Henry in 2017. They are expecting a girl in 2020.

Number two: Sing married Manikhone Khamvongsa. They have three sons: Kevin in 1993, and a set of twins, Michael and Victor, in 1995.

Number three: Ott married Terri Jansen. They have three children: Jason in 1985, Angela in 1994, and Justin in 2000. Jason married Robin Toohey, and they have two daughters, Macy in 2012 and Ivy in 2017. Angela married Clayton Roll.

Number four: Tay married Aimee Rabe.

Number five: Nang married Somlith Soudavanh. They have three children: Sofia in 1998, Raymond in 2000, and Manola in 2003.

Number six: Tee married Tom Rowden.

Number seven: Tow married Savarn Rose Vath. They have two children: Jessalena in 2003 and Jaydon in 2006.

Number eight: Noi married Tenille Bushmeyer. They have three children: Logan in 1998, Isabella in 1999, and Brooks in 2006.

I am so very thankful that Mom has left her forwarding address for where she is now, and we can all join her if we choose to. I have such peace to know that she is in heaven and has a new body with no more pain. She has no tears, no sorrow.

Leaving Laos took great faith. When I decided to go to Thailand, Mom and I made the decision, but I went first. Everyone else in our family followed. Mom and I are still the leaders in choosing where we will spend eternity, but this time Mom went ahead to heaven and is waiting there for me and whoever else accepts Jesus. On our first trip from Laos to Thailand, the family did not have to follow me, but they did. Leaving Laos worked out quite well for all of us here in our earthly lives. I pray that my loved ones will trust my instinct to follow me one more time and choose to follow me to heaven, where they would one day join Mom and me, and perhaps even Nang, for an eternal family reunion.

DAD SIBLINGS
MISSING#2CHILD
AUNT CHOUM

#1CHOUNG

#3HOM

#4 CHOM

#5HOUM-DAD

My mom's parents and siblings

Song and Houay Boualavong

#1 mom

#2 aunt Boualasy

#3 uncle Seng

#4 uncle Sisay

#5 aunt Tiane

#6 aunt Luckmany

#7 uncle Soutchay

#8 uncle Khamla

1-KHAM FAMILY

2-SING FAMILY
AT ANGELA'S WEDDING

3-OTT FAMILY

4-TAY FAMILY

5-NANG FAMILY&JOHN

6-TEE FAMILY

6-TOW FAMILY

8-NOI FAMILY

Aunt Boualasy
and me
My God's mother

Khamma and Lop
My parents'
matchmakers

Veng and me

Aunt Luckmany and Me
Aunt Luck and Veng escaped with me

Laura Doran

Chris Nagel

David Little

Some of our family's sponsors

Bob & Margaret Turner

Grace Oakley

Rev. Clifford & Opal

Neal & Margaret Jo
with our family

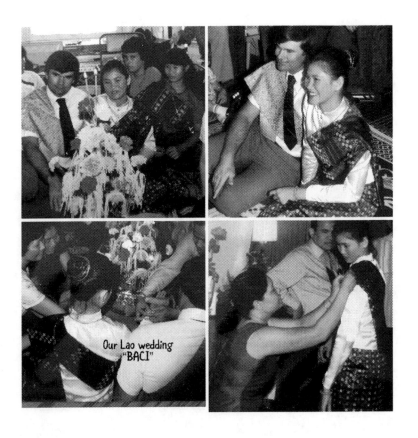

Our Lao wedding
"BACI"

Our wedding
July 9, 1983

Kham age 13
Kengkok, Laos

Kham age 17
Ubon, Thailand

Kham age 19
Quincy, IL

Carl and Kham

Sept 1, 2018
My niece Angela Sonethongkham's
Wedding

Lao dance
"Lamvong"

My sister Nang &
Her husband Lith

Carl and Kham family

#1 John

#2 Nathan

#3 Nolan

Acknowledgments

My family and so many other families will forever be thankful to Thailand for agreeing to provide a safe place for us to live while we applied to other countries to get legal permission to enter and reside there. We entered Thailand illegally. The country had every right to deport us back to our homeland. In this case, Dad would have been back in the hands of Laos Issara and would have been executed for his crime of disloyalty to their regime. However, the Thai people showed mercy to neighboring oppressed countries by offering us safe haven in refugee camps. Thailand created several camps along the Mekong River and other borders. I know Ubon Camp provided safety for Laotians from the southern part of the country, and northern Laos refugees had a refugee camp farther north. Other camps offered safety to refugees from Cambodia and Burma (Myanmar). All the refugees knew we would never be granted Thai citizenship, but Thailand allowed us to stay there to apply for a country to accept us legally.

My parents deserve the highest praise I can offer for their undying love and self-sacrifice to bring us to America and a better life. Mom always contributed to our finances but often had to be the total provider while Dad was away. She used her connections to plan and successfully execute our escape to the refugee camp, serving as our brave leader from Laos to Thailand. Dad, however, took over from Thailand to the United States. We all trusted

Dad's knowledge and intuition as he pushed for us to somehow get to America, and he did not let us down. Mom and Dad both encouraged us to get good educations and to be productive citizens. Thank you, both.

My maternal grandparents were very important to our family's well-being as they watched us and helped us when my parents had to be away from the home. Also, thank you, Uncle Seng and Aunt Sourivanh. Without Uncle Seng's help, our family would never have had a chance to grow up together. Aunt Sourivanh supported him, even though at times he was placing himself in extreme risk. I also thank Uncle Sisay, Aunt Bouakeo, Uncle Prasane, and Aunt Tiane for helping us financially while we were in the refugee camp. Our lives were much more secure because of their generosity.

I want to thank the First Presbyterian Church of Quincy, Illinois, for their unwavering support of my family throughout the years. They gave me my first glimpse of the love of Christ.

Neil and Margaret Jo Kurfman, Carl's late parents, provided so much for me and for my family. Neal, especially, would not give up on me. They saw value in a refugee girl who did not know Jesus, and they welcomed me and all my family into their lives.

As Rev. Clifford Phillips drove me from Quincy to Fishhook each week, he kindly and patiently guided me toward Jesus, especially when he explained the difference between following a man and following Jesus. Though he went to be with the Lord in 2013, I want to give credit to him and his sweet wife, Opal, for being so instrumental in my early faith.

For thirty-five years, the Fishhook UB Church has been blessed to have Pastor Mark Dickerson and his wife, Cheryl, lead the congregation. Mark and Cheryl have hearts to serve and teach the church family, and I have learned so much from their loving leadership.

Though I left my original home and everyone I knew there, Fishhook United Brethren Church became my new home for many reasons. Here, Carl and I had several role models of Christ-filled families. They continually prayed for my salvation and for all my family's welfare. They welcomed me with open arms and loved me as their own while Carl and I raised our children there. After I lost my only biological sister, I drew even closer to my church sisters in Christ. I am forever grateful to this group of God-fearing Christians.

I would like to thank several individuals for their help in the production of this book. I know many have prayed for the Holy Spirit to lead me, especially as I shared my testimony.

I appreciate Brenda Harrington for generously offering to financially support my book's publication. Brenda is my coauthor's sister, and she was following our book writing experience, praying for us all the way through. She loves the Lord and believes that my testimony will help sow the seed of salvation.

Linda Pearson, my coauthor, is Carl's cousin, but also a sister in Christ. We are good friends who have attended church and Bible study together for years, and we have children the same age. However, writing my life story has brought us even closer. Linda had never written a book before, but she was willing to give it a try after retiring from a thirty-four-year career of teaching English and language arts.

The first attempt to document my life story was a group effort. Kevin Henthorn is Carl's first cousin and his three daughters, Grace, Faith, and Emily, helped me to begin thinking about what my book would include. In the summer of 2016, their mother, Christine, was battling leukemia, taking treatments in St. Louis. Linda and I helped take over Christine's homeschooling duties while she was away. For a writing project, we planned to have the girls write about my life, so the girls began to interview me. Many of my early memories were recorded during these interviews. Once Christine recovered and was able to resume homeschooling, Linda and I set the project aside for a while. Eventually, we decided to get out those old notes and resume the project. From this point on, Linda and I were the writers.

Several people have helped edit and proofread for clarity. In particular, I would like to thank Kathy and Dave Dyer for helping research the chapter about my early faith. Also, Amanda Hurd, Nathan Kurfman, Carrie Bradshaw, and Debbie Niederhauser offered helpful suggestions to make the information clearer.

Tay and Ott contributed valuable information by sharing their stories of their separate journeys to Thailand. We were so fortunate to already have Nang's essay to provide memories of the fourth and final group's journey from Laos. What a blessing to have this in print for our children and our children's children!

I am extremely indebted to my niece, Sofia Soudavanh, for creating a helpful map to document my family's travels. Nang would be very proud of her eldest child today.

My husband, Carl, has loved me unconditionally and nurtured me as my faith began to grow. From the beginning of our relationship, Carl's only nondebatable request of me was to attend church with him, and there the seeds of my faith were planted. Carl was the gardener tending the seed in my heart. He has always kept me grounded in my faith, putting God and family first. Thirty-five years later, he is still my rock. Amen!

For years, when anyone asked me about my journey from Laos to Fishhook, I would share bits and pieces of the story. I heard over and over again, "You need to write a book." Thank you to every individual who planted these seeds and who prayed for this book to be produced. Without this encouragement to get started and the positive feedback during the writing, I might have put the project on the shelf and never finished it. Praise the Lord for answered prayer!

Above all, I want to thank God for the Good News—His offer of eternal life in heaven to all who believe through the sacrifice of His Son, Jesus Christ, our Lord and Savior.

Printed in the United States
By Bookmasters